THE YEAR MADE HOLY

THE YEAR
MADE HOLY

By Monsignor Matthias Premm

Translated from the German by COLMAN J. O'DONOVAN

THE BRUCE PUBLISHING COMPANY • *Milwaukee*

NIHIL OBSTAT:

    JOHN F. MURPHY, S.T.D.
    Censor librorum

IMPRIMATUR:

    ✠ WILLIAM E. COUSINS
    Archbishop of Milwaukee

    February 23, 1961

First published in English in 1958 by the Mercier Press Limited, 17 Drawbridge Street, Cork, Ireland. Published in Austria under the title Geheiligtes Jahr *by Verlag Herder, Vienna.*

Library of Congress Catalog Card Number: 61–13004

© 1961 THE BRUCE PUBLISHING COMPANY

MADE IN THE UNITED STATES OF AMERICA

FOREWORD

UNDER the title *The Holy Sacrifice* the author published in 1946 (Verlag Pustet, Salzburg) an explanation of the nonvarying texts of the Mass (*Ordinary of the Mass*). In one year 10,000 copies were sold. Exiled priests translated the booklet into the Hungarian and Croat languages. In the present book the variable texts of the liturgy of all the Sundays and feast days of the ecclesiastical year are likewise explained.

The explanation of the texts takes the form of a solemn liturgical homily. The texts of a feast day or a Sunday, as the case may be, are elucidated liturgically and devotionally in the order in which they stand in the Missal (*Introit, Collect, Epistle, Gradual, Gospel, Offertory hymn, Communion hymn*), but under one single main head, namely the basic thought of the day in question. This thought is also now and again brought out in the second chapter heading. In unity lies strength. The author is indebted for many ideas to the works of B. Baur (*Let there be Light*), Pius Parsch (*The Year of Salvation*), and to the *Way of Life* (Linz).

As to the practical utilization of the book: in the case of a Low Mass, instead of the customary meditation, the user must read over and reflect on, beforehand, the exposition for the relevant day. He will then follow the Holy Mass with far more benefit than if he had not made this preparation. In the case of a longer Service, however, it will be sufficient perhaps to read the commentary during the Service.

Whoever joins in this way in the Masses of all the feast days and Sundays of the ecclesiastical year will assist at them with an understanding of the Holy Mass that grows from year to year and in the true spirit of the liturgy. Every year will be for him *a year made holy*.

MATTHIAS PREMM

Salzburg, Marian Year, 1954

CONTENTS

viii   CONTENTS

THE YEAR MADE HOLY

THE ECCLESIASTICAL YEAR

THE liturgical celebration of the Eucharistic Rite requires not only its special place, which for that reason is called the House of God (church), but also its special time. Through it both place and time are sanctified. As regards time, we know that in the earliest days of the Church the Sacrifice of the Mass was offered in public on Sunday, the day of the resurrection. In this way every Sunday became a little Easter Sunday. Naturally the actual anniversary of the resurrection of Jesus was celebrated with special solemnity, and was preceded by a longer period of preparation. Thus the feast of Easter, which we know to have existed as far back as the second century, became the heart and center of the ecclesiastical year.

In the fourth century the commemoration of the birth of Christ, our feast of Christmas, was instituted. And so we still today divide the ecclesiastical year into two parts: the cycle of Christmas and the cycle of Easter. Pentecost and the Sundays after Pentecost are thoroughly paschal in spirit and have the character of an echo of the Easter cycle of feasts. Accordingly, the *Life of Jesus* from His birth to His resurrection, ascension, and finally the sending down of the Holy Spirit, constitutes the main thought of the ecclesiastical year. The year begins with Advent, a looking *to* and preparation *for* the incarnation of the Son of God at Christmas. After the few feast days which complete the cycle of Christmas feasts we come to the season of Lent, a time of preparation for the redemptive death of Christ and His ascension into heaven. That is the Easter cycle of feasts, and it includes not only the five Sundays after Easter, the Ascension into heaven, and the sending of the Holy Spirit at Pentecost, but also the twenty-four Sundays after Pentecost. The meaning of it is this: that what the Christian received at Easter in Baptism, Mass, Communion, and Confirmation he must preserve by struggle and prayer until the second coming of Christ on the last day, to which our thoughts are turned on the last Sunday after Pentecost. The man of Easter must prove himself in his everyday life.

Thus the ecclesiastical year is nothing less than a yearly re-living of the life Jesus once lived on earth; it is a *Year of the Lord*. By that very fact it is also a *Year of Salvation*, for we commemorate in the course of the year the various works of Jesus for our redemption and make them our own. We let ourselves be drawn into these holy events: we sacrifice ourselves with Christ, we die with Him in spirit, and cast off our sinful humanity in order that we may rise again transfigured with Christ and prepare ourselves for our own ascension into heaven. In very truth, a year made holy!

And then, how wonderfully does the Holy Spirit direct the liturgy of the Church! Just as, in general, our supernatural life is interwoven with the natural, so, too, the ecclesiastical year fits itself into the orbit of the calendar year. In the natural world the course of the seasons is determined by the path of the sun, the source of light and life. In like manner, Christ, who has described Himself as the "Light of the World" and as "Life," is the sun of our supernatural life of grace. Thus the religious ecclesiastical year and the natural sun year follow parallel courses. The ecclesiastical year begins with the season of Advent, when the sun is at its lowest, when the greater part of the twenty-four-hour day is veiled in darkness and the earth lies in the numbing grip of snow and ice. At this season the natural creature longs for light and new life. But the devout soul, in the season of Advent, longs for Christ and prays that He may redeem it from the darkness and rigidity of death. And when later the sun passes its nadir and once more turns its face toward the earth, then, too, the Church rejoices at the birth of the rising sun that is Christ. Christmas is decidedly a feast of light. In a little while, under the ever growing influence of the sun, new life begins to quicken in the womb of the earth, though it still has to contend with the hostile forces of cold and ice. It is here that we have the fasting time of Lent, the time of the struggles of Christ and of all Christians against the powers of evil. On Good Friday it would almost seem that Christ has succumbed before the might of Satan. At the death of Jesus the sun is darkened, but only to shine out all the more radiantly on Easter morning. The joyful feast of the Resurrection of Jesus coincides with the triumphant coming of spring, when all nature awakens to a new life. Then, as we approach the splendor of summer and the zenith of the sun's ascent, we celebrate the

Ascension of Christ into heaven, and Pentecost, the feast of the Holy Spirit who kindles in our hearts the torch of love, that our soul may come to its full ripening. Into this period, too, falls Corpus Christi, the feast of the unleavened Holy Bread that nourishes the soul to eternal life. Once more the sun begins to sink in the heavens. The granaries are stocked with grain and fruit. Next our thoughts turn to Mary, the Mother of God, and to her assumption, body and soul, into heaven, the richest golden sheaf of all. When at last, in the late autumn, the fields and gardens have all been harvested, the Church too celebrates its harvest, the Feast of All Saints, as a spiritual harvest thanksgiving. The commemoration of All Souls follows directly; these are the souls who have died in the Lord and are ripening for the harvest of their resurrection. And so the ecclesiastical year comes imperceptibly to a close and glides into the new Advent. The cycle of the natural and the spiritual year is completed and can begin afresh.

That is surely a wonderful drama, at once divine and human, "a poem of the Holy Ghost that year after year stirs our heart anew" (Otto Mauer).

But how many Christians live through the ecclesiastical year as in a half-sleep, with no proper realization of its grandeur! The present little book aims at rousing these liturgically tepid souls from their slumber. It tries to bring to life before their eyes the beauty of the texts of the Mass for the feast days of the Lord and the ordinary Sundays of the year, and thus stimulate them to a conscious participation in the ecclesiastical year.

And how fruitful this participation in the life of the Church can be! Each year will add another ring of union with Christ and His Church to the tree of the soul. By following, Sunday after Sunday, the liturgical texts of the Mass with full understanding we shall perfect ourselves more and more in the teachings of our faith and make ourselves strong in virtue, in sanctity, and in love of the Holy Church. That is what one may truly call Christian piety! In uninterrupted flow, light and life stream from the eucharistic Christ into our soul, which constantly expands in grace and holiness. The Christian who is devoted to the liturgy grows without noticing his growing; he "shall flourish like the palm tree, like a cedar of Lebanon shall he grow. They that are planted in the house of the Lord shall flourish in the courts of our God" (Ps. 91:13–14).

FIRST SUNDAY OF ADVENT

Yearning for Redemption

WE ENTER today on the season of Advent. The name is derived from the Latin *adventus* and means "coming," that is, the coming of Christ, the Redeemer. We must, however, distinguish between the various "comings" of Christ. In the popular mind the season before Christmas is associated only with the coming of the Child Jesus in Bethlehem nearly two thousand years ago. But, to the remembrance of the first coming of Jesus, the liturgical prayers of the Church during this season add the thought of His second coming for the last judgment at the end of the world and of His present continuous coming to our hearts through divine grace. In the texts of the Mass each of these thoughts is expressed in turn, and one could not hope to understand the liturgy of the Church if one thought solely of the first coming of Jesus at His birth in Bethlehem. That would certainly not be sharing the life of the Church in the season of Advent.

❖   ❖   ❖

The central theme of the liturgy of the Mass of the First Sunday of Advent is inner longing for the redemption, and that in a well-defined threefold sense. First, we call to mind the eager expectation of the exalted men and women of the Old Testament, such as an Isaias, and their prayers for the first coming of the Redeemer in Bethlehem. But since, for us, this has in fact come to pass, we yearn also for the coming of Jesus into our hearts through His gifts of grace, and for His last coming on the day of judgment. By the first coming of Jesus at the incarnation our redemption is prepared; by its merciful working in our hearts it is ensured and by the last judgment it is finally realized and accomplished.

And so we now approach the altar with hearts full of yearning for the Redeemer and the redemption. But, as we do so, we think — as always at the Holy Mass — not only of ourselves but also of our brothers and sisters who stand in need of redemption. We take

4

our place in their ranks, and pray for them too in their moral and spiritual need for mercy and deliverance. We do so at the outset in the prayers before the altar, when in the *Confiteor*, with one voice we acknowledge our sinfulness. Then, conscious of our own necessities and full of trust in God, we lift up our souls in the *Introit:* "To thee, O Lord, have I lifted up my soul. In thee, O my God, I put my trust; let me not be ashamed. Neither let my enemies laugh at me; for none of them that wait on thee shall be confounded. Show, O Lord, thy ways to me, and teach me thy paths!"

It will soon be two thousand years since the coming of the Redeemer. Many a time, too, has He come into our hearts at Holy Communion and through His divine grace. Nevertheless we have not all of us yet been fully redeemed. Countless numbers of our brothers and sisters live in sin, and many of them are not interested in a Redeemer. These are the neediest of all. And even we who flatter ourselves perhaps that we are free from mortal sin are over and over again made conscious of our proneness to evil, and of our lukewarmness and indifference to good. And so, in earnest yearning for full redemption we cry *Kyrie eleison!* And, chastened by the realization of our need of deliverance, we do not sing the joyful *Gloria*.

Today our *Collect*, which we address direct to Christ our Redeemer, is vehement, not to say stormy: "Stir up thy might, O Lord, we beseech thee, and *come;* that by thy protection we may deserve to be rescued from the threatening dangers of our sins and saved by thy deliverance." The suppliant "come" makes of this prayer a true Advent petition.

The *Epistle* is equally vehement. St. Paul wishes to rouse the Christians from their tepidity and their sleep of sin by reminding them of the day of Christ, that is to say His coming for the judgment. "Brethren, it is now the hour for us to rise from sleep. The night is passed, and the day [of Christ] is at hand. Let us therefore cast off the works of darkness, and put on the armor of light. Let us walk honestly, as in the day [as if the last judgment lay immediately ahead]; not in rioting and drunkenness, not in chambering and impurities, not in contention and envy. But put ye on the Lord Jesus Christ." That holds good not only for sinners, but also for those who say their daily prayers and go to Holy

Communion and so on. In ourselves, too, how much lukewarmness, carelessness, and slackness do we not find! We must rather, "put on the Lord Jesus Christ": in humility, purity, love of God and of our neighbor, in gentleness, patience, and readiness to suffer. Let that be our resolution for Advent. Let us ask for this grace as a Christmas gift from the Infant Jesus.

That our request will be hearkened to, we have the assurance of the *Gradual:* "None of them that wait on thee [on thy second coming] shall be confounded, O Lord. Show, O Lord, thy ways to me, and teach me thy paths." Confidently then we sing the joyful Alleluia, and, filled with expectation, we look to the coming of the Judge in the clouds of heaven: "Alleluia. Show us, O Lord, thy mercy, and grant us thy salvation. Alleluia." Then, in the *Gospel,* Christ Himself speaks to us, as on the last Sunday of the ecclesiastical year, of His coming for the judgment on the last day. In the liturgy of Advent this coming is even more stressed than His first coming in Bethlehem.

At the *Consecration* the Savior graciously condescends to come to us. That is His coming in compassion and grace. In the *Communion hymn* He comes into our hearts, just as formerly at His first coming He implanted Himself in the virgin womb of Mary. (Very apposite is the ceremony that takes place today in the station church of St. Mary Major in Rome.) What was once fulfilled in Mary is fulfilled in us today: "The Lord will bestow his benefits, and our earth shall yield its fruits" (*Communion hymn*). May the soil of our soul be daily so filled with new graces that the yearning for God shall grow in us unceasingly — until the day of final redemption at our death and at the last judgment!

SECOND SUNDAY OF ADVENT

The Redeemer Shall Come! Prepare Ye for His Coming!

ON THE First Sunday of Advent we acknowledged the great necessity of our soul, our need of redemption. Accordingly we prayed earnestly that the Savior might come. Today's Mass answers: Yes, your longing prayer shall be heard; the Redeemer shall come; prepare your soul to receive Him! Thus we have an intensification of the spirit of Advent.

In Rome there is celebrated today a special service in the Church of the Holy Cross in Jerusalem. Hence, in the texts of today's Mass we repeatedly meet with the word *Jerusalem,* or, as the case may be, Sion. We may read this in our prayers as meaning our soul. To it the Savior will come; in it He will shine out with a great brightness in the season of Christmas and later at the judgment.

"People of Sion, [my soul] behold the Lord shall come! He shall save the nations. And the Lord shall make the glory of his voice to be heard in the joy of your heart" (*Introit*). In the *Kyrie eleison,* as on the previous Sunday, we beseech the Lord to come soon and save us.

But we must prepare ourselves for this coming. Therefore, in the *Collect* we pray: "stir up our hearts, O Lord, to prepare the ways of thine only-begotten Son; that through his coming we may be worthy to serve thee with purified minds."

How to prepare ourselves we learn in the two lessons which now follow from St. Paul in the *Epistle* and from John the Baptist in the *Gospel.*

The *Epistle* lays stress on charity toward our neighbor as a means of preparation. "Be of one mind toward one another; that with one mind, and with one mouth, you may glorify God and the Father of Our Lord Jesus Christ. Wherefore receive one another, as Christ also hath received you." It is appropriate that these words should be addressed to us just at this solemn hour. In the Holy Sacrifice of the Mass we glorify God, but we glorify Him only if we really offer it in holy unison, if we really love one another, without excluding anyone from our all-embracing love. At the end of the Epistle Paul announces the coming of the Redeemer in the words: "There shall be a root of Jesse."

Filled with joy at this message, we sing in the *Gradual:* "Out of Sion [our soul] shines the loveliness of his beauty; God shall come manifestly." On this Sunday morning, we behold as it were the rising of the eternal sun. "Gather ye together his saints to him, who have set his covenant before sacrifices." Now, at the Holy Sacrifice, the light of God will shine in our soul, as later it will shine from the manger at Christmas and again when the Redeemer comes down from heaven in great power and majesty — for the judgment. "Alleluia! I rejoiced at the things that were said to me: we shall go into the house of the Lord [now the church, later the manger]! Alleluia!"

In the *Gospel* we meet with John, the precursor of Jesus, whom Jesus Himself describes as the prophet and the preparer of His way: John "is he of whom it is written, Behold I send my angel before thy face, who shall prepare thy way before thee." In the time of the Roman Empire, whenever the Emperor gave notice of his intention to visit a city — the visit itself was called an epiphany — preparations were made for months beforehand, houses were decorated, streets were leveled and cleaned. In like manner did John at the Jordan notify his people of the coming of the Redeemer. "Do penance, make straight his paths!" All the ruts in our way of life must be filled in, all excrescences removed, that there may be a smooth path for the coming Redeemer. The idea of penance is an essential part of the season of Advent: repentance for our sins and a firm resolve to avoid all sin in future. John himself gave us the example of a great penitent and it is as such that Jesus describes him in the *Gospel* of today. Like John, let us too not be "as a reed," blown helplessly back and forth by the breath of public opinion and by every gust of passion. Like him, let us too, not "clothe ourselves in soft garments," always seeking what is comfortable and enjoying what is pleasant.

There is no need to wait for the feast of Christmas: let us here and now, at the gracious coming of the Redeemer at the *Consecration,* prepare ourselves in this spirit of repentance. Let us picture ourselves as the blind, the lame, the lepers, the deaf, who are referred to at the beginning of the *Gospel.* And, in truth, how blind we are in what concerns our salvation! How lame, in that we advance so painfully in holiness! How leprous, that is to say unclean, in our thoughts and in the motives of our actions! How deaf to God's teachings! Many of us perhaps spiritually dead, being without the life of sanctifying grace. Let us therefore, now at the *Consecration,* implore the Redeemer to guard us from all these miseries and to cure us of all our infirmities. Let us recite from our hearts the *Offertory hymn:* "Turn, O God, and bring us to new life, and thy people shall rejoice in thee: show us, O Lord, thy mercy, and grant us thy salvation."

And truly the gentle Savior, the friend of humble sinners, comes to us now in the Holy Sacrifice, into our very hearts. "Arise, O Jerusalem [Christian soul], and stand on high: and behold the joy that cometh to thee from thy God" (*Communion hymn*). And as He unites Himself with us today, so will He come too at the hour of our death, as Judge it is true, but also to conduct us into the joy of heaven. Then shall be realized in the fullest measure the words: "Behold the joy that comes to you from your God!"

THE IMMACULATE CONCEPTION
(DECEMBER 8)

"Thou Art All Fair, Full of Grace"

EVERY feast of Mary portrays for us some glorious attribute of the Mother of God. In today's feast Mary is presented, not as the Mother with the Child, nor as the Mother of Sorrows, nor as the Queen of Heaven, but as Mary the Immaculate, the stainless. The texts of today's Mass all represent Mary in the first instant of her being adorned with grace, and by reason of that fact, free from original sin. Original sin, the privation of sanctifying grace, is the punishment for the sin of Adam, our first parent. Had Adam not sinned, then all his descendants would have entered on their lives in the full beauty of grace. But as things are we are conceived without grace in our mother's womb, and are on that very account displeasing and without beauty in the eyes of God, since the grace that should be in us is lacking. Only subsequently do we attain grace through the sacrament of baptism. In the case of Mary alone did God make an exception, because she was to be His mother: from the very first instant when her soul was created in the womb of her mother, Anna, she was already arrayed in sanctifying grace, and this to an extraordinary degree. That is the basic thought of today's feast.

This thought is expressed at the outset in the magnificent *Introit* which overflows with gladness and jubilation. Mary herself stands before us and, filled with gratitude to God, says: "I will greatly rejoice in the Lord, and my soul shall be joyful in my God; for he hath clothed me [at the very beginning of my being] with the garments of salvation, and with the robe of justice he hath covered me, as a bride adorned with her jewels. I will extol thee, O Lord, for thou hast upheld me, and hast not made my enemies to rejoice over me [through original sin]. Glory be to the Father, Son and Holy Spirit!" Yes, truly, on this day Mary has every reason to rejoice in the Lord and to sing a hymn of praise to the Holy Trinity. For to her alone of all the millions of beings of all the ages has this great privilege fallen. And we too should rejoice with Mary, for she is our mother, and it would be an unnatural child that did not rejoice in his heart at an honor done to his mother.

But when we turn our gaze from the shining form of Mary to look upon ourselves, we humbly bow our head and pray: *Kyrie Eleison!* From the first moment of our existence up to our baptism we carried the stain of original sin. It is true that we have not to repent of our original sin as of a sin that we ourselves have committed, but nevertheless we are saddened by the thought that at that moment instead of being pleasing in the eyes of God we were rather children of His "wrath." Let us see to it that at the end of our days, at least, we shall go sinless out of this world to God. That is what we pray for in the *Collect* of today: Grant that by the intercession of Mary, the Immaculate, we too may come with clean hearts to Thee.

Moreover, this special privilege had been predestined by God for His mother from the beginning of time, as we see in the Book of Wisdom (Chapter 8). Yes, the plans of God, which in the course of the ages He fulfills, were made in eternity. When, long before anything outside Himself existed, He conceived the plan of man's redemption through His Son, there was also present before His eyes the woman who was to be the mother of His Son. From time everlasting God had looked with special favor upon Mary, and prepared wonderful things for her, in particular a great fullness of grace at the moment of her conception. That is the theme of the first Lesson of today's Mass. As in the *Introit,* here too Mary speaks to us herself: "The Lord possessed me in the beginning of his ways, before he made anything, from the beginning. I was set up from eternity, and of old before the earth was made. The depths were not as yet, and I was already conceived [in God's plan]. When he prepared the heavens I was present. When he compassed the sea with its bounds, and set a law to the waters that they should not pass their limits, I was with Him" [in thought before the eye of God]. Already in the first plans that God had in view for His world, Mary had an important role as mother of the Redeemer of mankind. Even then, because of the unique part she was to play in the plan for the salvation of mankind, God had decided to preserve Mary from original sin and to adorn her with grace from the very first instant. God Himself — in His own mind — painted the first and most beautiful Madonna; He was Himself, if one may say so, the first votary of the Virgin Mary, as the present Lesson shows. No one therefore has any right to find fault with us if we poor mortals, too, render sincere honor to our Lady. At the end of the Lesson from the Old Testament Mary addresses to us the gracious words: "[My] children, hear me. Blessed are they that keep my ways. Blessed is the man that heareth me and that watcheth daily at my gates. He that shall find me shall find life and shall have salvation from the Lord." Such is the blessing that comes from a devout honoring of Mary.

In the texts of today's Mass up to this point the Church has presented the Immaculate to us, and Mary herself has spoken to us. Charmed with this delightful picture we now sing with full hearts at the *Gradual*: "O Virgin Mary, blessed art thou of the Lord most high above all the women of the earth. Thou art the glory of Jerusalem [the Church]. Thou art all fair, O Mary, and the original stain of sin is not in thee. Alleluia!" Certainly there are to be found among the other saints many who during their entire lives have committed not only no mortal sin, but even hardly a single fully deliberate venial sin. They too are fair, but still not all fair, not one of them. For they all, in their mother's womb, carried in themselves the stain of original sin. Only Mary, as the future mother of the Son of God, was covered with grace from the first moment of her existence. Of all the children of men, Mary only and alone is all fair.

It is little wonder that not only we mortals, but also even the angels, should be enraptured with the timeless beauty of Mary, as we see in the *Gospel* of today's Feast, which tells how the Archangel Gabriel was sent by God to Mary at Nazareth. On other feast days of Mary, as well, we are told of this sending, but in much greater detail. Today's account is strikingly brief. It is confined to the greeting of the angel and says nothing of what followed, nothing of Mary's consent to the incarnation of the Son of God. The reason for this is that it is precisely this greeting of the angel that is most important for today's feast. For, the words of the angel, "Hail, full of grace," emphasize, so the Church teaches us, Mary's freedom from original sin. When the angel, at the behest of God, gives the greeting: "Hail, full of grace," he says exactly what the Church has said to Mary in the passage quoted: "Thou art all fair," for there is complete correspondence between the words all (fair) and full (of grace).

The sublime greeting of the angel continues to ring in our ears, for, in the *Offertory hymn,* the angelic salutation comes lovingly to our lips also as, gazing in rapt devotion on Mary, we pray: *Ave Maria, gratia plena.* We hail you, full of grace! You are full of the grace that was with you from the first moment. Truly, the Lord has been with you, ever blessed, chosen before all women in the history of the world. Already at the very first moment you possessed more grace than did any of the saints after a long life of holiness. Full of joy at the greatness and beauty of our Mother, today we add an Alleluia to the *Offertory* prayer.

Finally, at the *Communion,* the Church bids us turn once more to Mary and pray: "Glorious things are said of you, O Mary; for he that is mighty has done great things for you." Yes, truly wonderful are the things that the Church has expressed in these texts of today's feast day of Mary: that from the first moment of her existence she was bedecked with sanctifying grace as with precious bridal jewels, preordained for her from all eternity, that she might be the Immaculate, the all fair, the full of grace.

How great sanctifying grace must be! God, who can give all things, since all things belong to Him, must surely have given His mother for her bridal array the very best that it was in His power to give, and He knew nothing greater than the shining raiment of sanctifying grace. From this we see that, in the eyes of God, holiness, virtue, purity of soul are the most precious things of all, while in the eyes of men earthly possessions and material beauty are given the highest place. Let us therefore take home with us from today's Mass the resolution to see in sanctifying grace the highest good that we can obtain on earth. Through it we become children of God, pleasing in His sight, and acquire a title deed to heaven as our inheritance. Only those who possess the wedding garment of sanctifying grace can enter heaven. Up there, at the side of our heavenly mother, we too must be able to say of ourselves: "Truly great are the things that the Almighty hath done for me!"

THIRD SUNDAY OF ADVENT

The Redeemer Is Near! Rejoice!

IN HOW masterly a way the liturgy of the Church contrives to intensify the Advent spirit in us from week to week! On the first Sunday it awakened in us in a very general way a recognition of our need of redemption, and a yearning for the Redeemer. On the second Sunday it promised us: He shall come; prepare ye the way for Him! Today, the Third Sunday, the liturgy tells us: He is already near; therefore rejoice! Just as the children are already counting the days till the coming of the Christ Child at Christmas, so, in us adults too, should the joyful yearning for God increase from day to day in the last stages of Advent.

      ❈   ❈   ❈

Quiet, restrained joy is therefore the keynote of today's feast, and the liturgy adapts itself accordingly. The altar today is sparsely dressed with flowers. The organ plays. The Mass vestments are not violet but rose, a softening of the penitential violet. This basic harmony of holy joy appears in the *Introit* of the Mass, which is taken from the *Epistle:* "Rejoice in the Lord always, again I say, rejoice. Let your modesty be known to all men. The Lord is nigh." That is the first reason for our joy: The Lord is nigh. It is a holy joy, a joy in the Lord.

For this inner joy, then, we pray expressly in the *Collect.* For, just as outside in the world at this season darkness holds sway and the period of daylight is short, so too in our soul the light is all too dim. And so we pray — a true Advent prayer — that God Himself may come and bring light and joy to our soul: "Incline thine ear, O Lord, we beseech thee, to our prayers, and enlighten the darkness of our mind by the grace of thy visitation." Thus we pray, not to the Father, but directly to Christ, the Redeemer, who has told us that He is the Light of the World.

The *Epistle* now brings us to the central theme of the liturgy of today's Mass. We must give it, therefore, our closest attention. "Brethren! Rejoice in the Lord always . . . The Lord is nigh." It is joy, primarily, that the Apostle enjoins on us. And the reason: because "the Lord is nigh." He is near us now on the altar at the sacrifice of the Mass; constantly by day and night here in the tabernacle; and especially near, no within us, in Holy Communion. Yet all these are but transient moments. With His godhead, however, He is alway near. That is why Paul tells us that we must rejoice *always*. He is indeed ever present for us: "In Him we live, and move, and are" (Acts 17:28). Nay, in His love for us God has even taken up His abode in our hearts. Jesus Himself has given us that assurance: "If anyone love me, we [Father, Son, and Holy Spirit] will come to him, and make an abode with him" (Jn. 14:23). Truly, the Lord is near — and yet we know Him not, and think so little of His ever presence in us. Especially now in Advent we should think constantly of God's presence, for that is the inexhaustible spring of pure, holy joy. As St. Francis de Sales says: "How happy is the soul who in the stillness of his heart lovingly preserves the holy feeling of the presence of God." Joy is the essence of a healthy spiritual life.

But whoever is himself happy inevitably passes on some of his happiness to others. So Paul continues: "Let your modesty be known to all men. The Lord is nigh." By virtue of our own goodness will the Lord, whom we carry within us, overflow to our fellow men and bring them nearer to God. St. Theresa of the Child Jesus always had a kindly smile for everyone, but it was not just something that she had cultivated by careful practice; it sprang naturally from her own kindly, benevolent heart. We must see Jesus Himself also in our fellow man. In our neighbor Jesus Himself is always near, but alas we never think of that. At the last judgment

Jesus will hold us to account for it. "What you have done to one of these my least brethren, you did it to me."

"Be not solicitous," for God, who is so near you, will take away your cares if you pray to Him with confidence: "In everything, by prayer and supplication, with thanksgiving, let your petitions be made known to God." "If God be for us [lovingly abides in us], who is against us?" (Rom. 8:31.) Who can then harm us? "To them that love God, all things work together unto good" (Rom. 8:28).

In this way, deeply spiritual Christians live in a perpetual peace, in a quiet happiness of which worldly men have no conception. The *Epistle* speaks of this toward the end: "And the peace of God, which surpasseth all understanding, keep your hearts and minds in Christ Jesus." Joy, goodness, holy unconcern, peace of heart because God is so near to us — these are the thoughts that the liturgy of the Church offers today for our encouragement.

But even in the most faithful Christian the happiness of the perceptible nearness of God does not always reign. Days and weeks may come, when we feel ourselves completely abandoned by God. Let us at such moments seek Him, filled with the Advent yearning, and call out to Him as in the *Gradual* of today: "Stir up thy might, O Lord, and come to save us! Alleluia!"

It happens to us at times as happened to the Jews in the time of John the Baptist (*Gospel*): they yearned for the Redeemer and sought Him in John, thinking he was He. Whereupon the forerunner of the promised Messias had to say to them sharply: "He stands already in your midst — and you know him not." The unbelieving world will not accept Christ, who has been in their midst for close on two thousand years, as the Redeemer; nor does it believe that He is present in the Most Holy Sacrament, especially now in the Holy Sacrifice of the Mass. We Christians believe it, and that is why we assist at the divine service. But it is yet faith only: we long to be able to see Christ face to face.

We know, of course, that through the death of Christ on the cross we have already been redeemed, and we express our thanks for it in the *Offertory hymn:* "Lord, thou hast blessed thy land . . . [and] hast forgiven the iniquity of thy people." But, for all that, the redemption of each one of us individually has not yet been accomplished, and as long as we remain on earth we have constant

need of forgiveness. We are not yet fully and finally united with
God. We can even lose this union by mortal sin. On the other hand
this union can and ought to become ever closer the longer we live.
Therefore we must pray unceasingly to God that we may abide
with Him. Our Advent yearning should last the whole of our lives.
Only when we close our corporeal eyes in the darkness of death and
our soul awakens in the bright and blissful and unending embrace
of God — only then shall we behold God face to face as the
shepherds beheld the Child in the manger. Then all the Advent
yearning will have ceased and the great and everlasting Christmas
will have dawned for us.

FOURTH SUNDAY OF ADVENT

Come, O Lord, and Do Not Delay!

THIS Sunday is a synthesis of the preceding Sundays of Advent.
On each Sunday up to now there has been more or less only one
Advent figure. On the first, Isaias, on the second, John the Baptist,
on the third, in a certain sense, Mary, for, with the incarnation in
her womb, the Redeemer was "already nigh," "in our midst," though
still unknown and hidden. Today we have before us as the three
figures of Advent: Isaias in the *Introit* with his cry: "Drop down
dew, ye heavens, from above!" — John in the *Gospel* with his injunction: "Prepare ye the way!" — Mary in the *Introit* and *Communion hymns.* Today's Mass bears a pronounced impress of Mary,
as is only to be expected. For already the Redeemer is stirring in
her womb and we are awaiting only the hour of His birth in the
manger and in our hearts.

❖   ❖   ❖

In the *Introit,* filled with yearning, we send up to heaven the
confident cry of Isaias: "Drop down dew, ye heavens, from above,
and let the clouds rain the just!" Heaven has, in fact, already
opened over Nazareth and the dew has already dropped down from

above: by the power of the Holy Spirit Mary has conceived our Savior and Redeemer. That part of our prayer has been answered. And now we pray that the second part may soon be answered too: "Let the earth be opened, and bud forth a Savior!" May the virgin womb of Mary give us soon the divine Child, that we may see and adore Him. Indeed, we ourselves too, and all Christians, are, in a sense, Mary. Of itself our soul is but hard, dry, and sterile soil. "My soul is as earth without water before thee, [O God]" (Ps. 142:6). We can only be saved (redeemed) when the dew of grace descends on us from above and divine life enters our soul. God is the heavenly light, we are the black earth. Only when He comes down and like the corn seed (in baptism) fructifies the soil of our sinful soul does there begin for us a new life that far transcends our natural life, and out of our soil the Savior is born; that is to say, a man renewed and pure and filled with the divine power, a God-man. What could the birth of Jesus in Bethlehem avail us if He were not also born in ourselves by the power of His grace?

In the *Collect* we earnestly pray that this may come about: "Stir up, O Lord, we pray thee, thy power, and *come*, and with great might succor us; that, by the help of thy grace, that which our sins impede may be hastened by thy merciful forgiveness." Only sin and our evil inclinations and habits stand in the way of our full redemption; that is why we pray for God's "merciful forgiveness." Like that of Mary, our soul too must be virgin-pure, at least through remorse and penance, if God is to unite Himself with it. A glorious Advent prayer, profound in its thought and vehement in its ardent emotion!

In the *Epistle*, once more, Paul speaks earnestly of the second coming of Christ at the judgment (at our death and on the last day). His warning is twofold: first, we must regard ourselves in our life on earth as merely stewards of the possessions and talents that God has entrusted to us. Later we shall have to render account to the Judge of the manner in which we have used the gifts and graces of God from day to day. "Brethren: let a man so account of us as of the ministers of Christ, and the dispensers of the mysteries of God. Here now it is required among the dispensers, that a man be found faithful." And the second warning: "Judge not before the time; until the Lord come [for the judgment], who both will bring to light the hidden things of darkness, and will make manifest the counsels of the hearts." In its essence this is no different from the warning of Jesus: "Judge not, and you shall not be judged" (Lk. 6:37). If we desire that Christ, on His second coming, shall be for us a merciful Judge, we too must be gentle in our judgment of others in this life. We must not be too quick to pass sentence on them, for often we do not know the inner motives which alone give the words or actions their merit or demerit. In the last days before Christmas everyone sets about cleaning up and decorating his house. Let us do this too with our souls.

Our sensibility of our imperfection enhanced by the *Lesson,* we send up, at the *Gradual,* our sighs to the Redeemer: "The Lord is nigh unto all them that call upon him. Alleluia! Come, O Lord, and do not delay; forgive the sins of thy people." In praying thus humbly and preserving ourselves from sin we are already obeying the injunction that John the Baptist addresses in the *Gospel* to us: "Prepare ye the way of the Lord. . . . Every valley shall be filled, and every mountain and hill shall be brought low."

In the *Offertory hymn* we salute Mary, in whose womb, as in a living monstrance, the Savior is already stirring: "Hail, Mary, full of grace; the Lord is with thee: blessed art thou among women, and blessed is the fruit of thy womb." Only in retrospect, of course, can we say the prayer, for it is a long time since Jesus stirred in her womb.

But at the *Consecration* He comes to us today. And to do so He puts forth — as in the *Collect* we begged Him to do — all His might, all His miraculous power in order to be with us mystically under the appearance of bread and wine.

And when in the *Communion hymn* we read: "Behold, a virgin shall conceive, and bear a son, and his name shall be called Emmanuel [God with us]," then, in that moment, we ourselves are truly Mary. For the same Savior has just come also to us, stirs in our hearts also with His manhood that He received from Mary. Would that He might find in us also the worthy heart that He once found in her: a heart full of purity and humility, free from all sin and all selfishness, and ready always and everywhere to submit utterly, even in suffering and sacrifice, to the most holy will of God, and to seek nothing on this earth but Him.

CHRISTMAS: THIRD MASS

"The Word Was Made Flesh"

WHAT we have yearned for all through the Advent season: "O come, Emmanuel [God with us]," has today been brought to fulfillment: the Eternal Son of God, the Word of the Father, has taken on, out of Mary the Virgin, our human nature, and "dwells among us" in the manger at Bethlehem. He is at once God and man, truly Emmanuel. Today, in its rejoicing, the Church allows three Masses, a thing that does not happen even at Easter, the greatest feast of the whole ecclesiastical year.

In masterly fashion the liturgy of the three Masses employs the motif of light. In the natural world outside the sun has reached its solstice; it begins to rise higher and higher and the days from now on will gradually become longer. For our soul, Christ is the sun that rises for us today. He who has called Himself the "Light of the World" has been born a child in the darkness of the night, with only Mary and Joseph to witness His coming. The *Gospel* of the first Mass records the external circumstances of His birth. At first the light shines only in the stable of Bethlehem, and then at dawn the shepherds appear, to greet the Child. For an angel had announced to them the birth of the Messias, the while "the brightness of God shone round about them." This thought is brought into relief at the second Christmas Mass in the so-called "Office of the Shepherds" beginning with the words: "A light shall shine upon us this day." From out the stable the light had shone forth, far over the plain of Bethlehem. Out of the night the dawn had come.

*   *   *

In the third Christmas Mass, the real festival Mass, we too, in fact the whole world, gather round the manger. "Come, ye gentiles, and adore the Lord" (*Alleluia*). The light that had begun to shine in the early morning has now become bright day and has spread itself over the earth. It shines in fact like bright sunshine over this Mass, in which everything is great, for in it we are paying homage to the little Child as the Lord of the World. That is the refrain of the whole liturgy of the Mass. In our Christmas folk songs we think more (though by no means solely) of the human attributes of the Child in the manger,° but the liturgy stresses rather the divine and aims at awakening in us deeper conceptions. Yet, even as the Child in the manger, Jesus is worthy of our adoration, for His human nature is not also a human person but belongs entirely to the divine Person of the Son of God Himself. We have here, not two persons, one human and one divine, but only the divine Person who has assumed our human nature.

The *Introit*, it is true, with its opening words "A child is born to us," evokes in our mind a picture of something small and lovable. But immediately it goes on — the Child thus "growing" in our sight to the divinely immeasurable — "the government [of the world] is upon his shoulder; and his name shall be called the Angel of great counsel." For this miracle of omnipotent goodness we give thanks to the Triune God: to the Father, "who gave for us His only-begotten Son"; to the Son, who was prepared to be the "Angel of great counsel," that is to say, to fulfill the plan of the redemption of the world; and to the Holy Spirit, who in the womb of Mary had worked this miracle: "Sing ye to the Lord a new canticle, for he hath done wonderful things."

Jubilantly, as in the *Gloria* that the angels sang at the time, we render homage to the Lord of the world who lies before us as a little child: "We praise thee, we adore thee. . . . Who sittest at the right hand of the Father, have mercy upon us. Thou only art holy, thou only, O Jesus Christ, art most high, together with the Holy Ghost, in the glory of God the Father."

In the *Collect*, which we address to the Father, our jubilation goes up in humble entreaty for redemption and deliverance from the slavery of sin: "Grant, we beseech thee, almighty God, that the new birth of thine only-begotten Son in the flesh may deliver us from the yoke of sin."

In the *Epistle* Paul approaches the manger and tells us of the hidden greatness of this frail child. In particular he refers to the world governance that "is upon his shoulder" (*Introit*): Jesus is the heir to the universe, while at the same time its creator. He is, as Son of God, as "mirror" of the Father, exalted far beyond the

° See German Christmas hymn *Silent Night*.

angels, so that they must adore Him even in His humanity notwithstanding that, on account of their own purely spiritual nature, they stand high above all ordinary human beings. His throne is for ever and ever; justice is His scepter; God Himself has anointed Him king of the world; His kingdom endures forever.

Thrilled by this message of the Apostle we sing in the *Gradual:* "Sing joyfully to God [the Child in the manger], all the earth. . . . Alleluia, alleluia. A sanctified day has shone upon us; come, ye gentiles, and adore the Lord: for this day a great light hath descended upon the earth. Alleluia."

In the *Gospel,* John, the theologian of the Evangelists, carries on the thoughts of Paul the Apostle and enlarges on them. This newborn child, as the immaterial Word innerly spoken by the Father, was with God and was Himself God. But in time, today too, He shines as the great light in the darkness of the world to illumine every man by His teaching and His grace. Many, to be sure, reject Him, will not hear of Him; but we, at least, bend our knee before Him today in childlike faith and proclaim: "The Word was made flesh and dwelt among us" — here in the manger. The Son of God became man, that we men might become children of God, brothers of Jesus, "born of God," as was He.

At the *Credo* we acknowledge further: "Jesus Christ, the only-begotten Son of God. Born of the Father before all ages. God of God; Light of Light; true God of true God. Begotten not made; of one being with the Father. Who for us men was incarnate by the Holy Ghost of the Virgin Mary, and was made man." These last words we say on our knees, because this very day they are to come to fulfillment.

In the *Offertory hymn* our adoring jubilation rings out anew: "Thine are the heavens [O Child in the manger], and thine is the earth: the world and the fullness thereof thou has founded; justice and judgment are the preparation of thy throne."

In what we have so far sung and heard and meditated we have gone back in spirit to the Child that lay in the manger more than nineteen hundred years ago. But at the *Consecration* Jesus comes to us in reality and renews Himself on the altar afresh: "And the Word was made flesh, and dwelt among us." "A child is born to us . . . and the government [of the world] is upon his shoulder." We are even permitted, though it be under the veil of the Sacrament, to take Him into our heart. At the *Communion* it is Christmas too in our hearts, and we offer it up to the Child in heartfelt love. May He set up His throne in us and reign as King forever!

SUNDAY AFTER CHRISTMAS

Children of God Through the Child Jesus

TODAY brings us a stage further in our understanding of the profound mystery of Christmas. On the feast itself the Child in the manger was alone the object of our adoring meditation. Today we ask ourselves: What gift does the Child bring us? And the liturgy answers: the adoption of God.

At the beginning of the Mass we go back in spirit once more to the Child in the manger. In the *Introit*, as on Christmas Day, we adore the incarnate Son of God, the eternal Word of the Father: "For while all things were in quiet silence, and the night was in the midst of her course, thy almighty word [O Lord], leapt down from heaven, from thy royal throne!"

In the *Collect* we implore of the Father that, through His Son, He may allow us to "abound in good works."

In the *Epistle* we are more fully informed as to what this "abounding in good works" consists in: the Child in the manger frees us of all oppression, and makes us children of God. God became man that we might become like unto God by sharing in the nature and life of God Himself. By the sin of Adam we lost the adoption of God and became slaves of passion, of the flesh, of lust, of the world, of sin, of Satan. And, for the period of the Old Testament, there was added the heavy yoke of the Mosaic law. "But when the fullness of the time came, God sent his Son, born of a woman," to liberate us from all these things and to make us adopted children of God, so that, with the Child in the manger, we may now address God by the tender name of Father and are even ourselves made heirs through God. The succoring grace of Christ helps us to overcome our evil and enslaving impulses. Sanctifying grace enables our soul to participate in the nature of God Himself, in the divine life of Jesus. His human nature is the vine upon which we are grafted, so that our soul pulsates with the life of the divine nature of Jesus, just as the grape draws life from the sap of the vine. Here is the supernatural life, the life in God, that Jesus has brought us. Even on earth it is ours. And after death we are admitted to God's domain and become heirs to the beatific life of God Himself. Filled with interior happiness at this magnificent Christmas gift, we turn once more, in the interval between the two Lessons, to the divine Child in the manger and sing in His honor a Christmas hymn (*Gradual*): "Thou art beautiful above the sons of men. . . . My heart hath uttered a good word. . . . Alleluia! The Lord [the Child in the manger] hath reigned, and hath girded himself with power."

The *Gospel* gives us warning that, despite the birth of the Son of God in the flesh, not all men become children of God and heirs to heaven, because not all are of good will. The Child in the manger is the Great Divide for the minds of all ages. On the one side are those who hate and persecute Christ, as Herod of old; on the other, those who love Him and become children of God, as all those of whom today's Gospel speaks: Mary, the most holy Mother of God, her chaste spouse, Joseph, the elderly Simeon, entirely dedicated to God and illumined by the Holy Ghost, and finally Anna, the chaste widow, who day and night gave herself to prayer and mortification. These are the new generation of the children of God, engendered by the grace of the Christ-Child. Thus are we too children of God and brethren of Jesus.

That is the inner meaning of the mystery of Christmas, as expressed also in the mixing of wine and water at the *Offertory* of the Mass: At first, in Adam, God created man's being "in a marvelous manner," that is to say, in a state of grace, as a child of God. Then, when Adam sinned and fell from grace both for himself and us, Jesus "in a manner still more marvelous" renewed our being, namely by assuming our human nature, thus making us sharers in His divine nature. That is why the priest, at the mixing of a drop of water (symbol of our weak human nature) with the wine (divine nature) offers the prayer: "Grant that through the mystery of this water and wine we may be made partakers of his divinity, who condescended to partake of our humanity, Jesus Christ, your Son, our Lord."

This mystery is now renewed in all reality at the Holy Mass. At the *Consecration*, "while all is still," the Word of God, wrapped in the veil of mystery, descends softly from His throne in heaven on to the altar, which has thus become the manger. At the *Communion* He unites Himself with us, filling our soul with His divine nature and making us children of God.

OCTAVE OF THE NATIVITY

Forward With Jesus, the Lord of Time, Into the New Year

LITURGICALLY, we celebrate today the Octave Sunday of Christmas. For this reason the hymns of the Mass, with the exception of the Alleluia verses, are all taken from the third Mass of Christmas. The Epistle is the same as that of the first Christmas Mass. It tells of the circumcision of Jesus which was performed on the eighth day after His birth. The calendar new year is not, of course, directly referred to in the liturgy, but nevertheless there is no reason why we should not relate the Mass texts to it. Is not Jesus the Lord of time?

When Jesus was born a new era began, the era of Christendom. All over the world time is reckoned according to the calendar from the year of the birth of Christ, and today we begin the nineteen-hundred-and-sixty-first year from the birth of Christ. And every time we begin a new year, Jesus lies once more as a Child in the manger, and blesses the new year. As Son of God, He is the Lord of time. In His tiny hands He grasps the spokes of the wheel of time. The great and proud may think that they make world history, but in reality it is the providence of God that guides the fate of mankind, the great events of the world and our individual destinies alike. "My journal for the coming year has long ago been written by God, down to its smallest detail" (Eberschweiler). In humble faith, and full of trust in God, let us pray to the Child in the manger that He may direct and guide our destiny too in the year that has just begun, and let us surrender ourselves utterly to His loving guidance.

In this spirit, in the *Introit,* we adore the Child Jesus in the manger: "A child is born to us, . . . and the government [of the world] is upon his shoulder; and his name shall be called . . . the Prince of Peace." We do not know what His counsels will bring us in the new year, but we welcome them lovingly whatever they may be. And so we write the name of Jesus right at the top of the first page of the new year, in submission to His holy will. We are resolved that the year shall be nothing less than a living "Glory be to the Father, the Son, and the Holy Spirit."

In the *Collect* we turn, filled with childlike confidence, to Mary, the mother of Jesus, who is our mother also and whose intercession procures for us all graces: "O God, who, by the fruitful virginity of blessed Mary, hast given to mankind the rewards of eternal salvation; grant, we beseech thee, that we may experience her intercession for us, through whom we have been made worthy to receive the author of life, Jesus Christ thy Son our Lord." And so, on the first page of the year, next to the name of Jesus, we inscribe the name of Mary.

In the *Epistle* Paul outlines the program for the new year, on the negative as well as on the positive side. On the negative side when he exhorts us to renounce our errors and lead a sinless life in the new year. We must give up "ungodliness and worldly desires." We must undergo a spiritual circumcision, cutting away the sproutings of evil which ever and ever grow again. We must reject the enticements of the world and of our senses. But even all this is not enough: we must also "do good works" in a positive way. We must, as the Apostle enjoins, "live soberly and justly and godly in the world." Our life must be modeled on Christ; our gaze, in this new year as at all times, must constantly be turned toward Christ, "looking for the blessed hope and coming of the glory of the great God and our Savior Jesus Christ." Today too there rises up before us the thought of the coming of Jesus at the judgment. It behooves us Christians to view everything we meet with in life in the light of eternity. We must repeatedly ask ourselves, with Aloysius: "How does this serve me for Eternity?"

The *Gospel* is the shortest of the whole year; it consists of just one sentence. But how pregnant that one sentence is! It tells us that even the Savior, on the eighth day after His birth, like all male infants of the Israelites, underwent the painful operation of circumcision, and that He was given the name of Jesus. Already as a newborn child He begins to shed His blood for us. Already He fulfills the meaning of His Name: Redeemer (of mankind), and begins to redeem us from our sins. The first blood that He sheds today is the earnest that at the end of His life He will give all His blood for us. Today He starts on the path of obedience — He is to be obedient unto death, unto death upon the cross. Even now the cross throws its shadow over the manger. God grant that we too, in the coming year, may show a like obedience to the will of God, ready, even to the bearing of suffering and sorrows, to co-operate in the redemption of mankind, filling up "those things that are wanting in the sufferings of Christ."

At the *Consecration* the same blood is present that once flowed at the Circumcision, and Jesus offers it to the heavenly Father in atonement for our sins of the past year.

At the *Communion* we unite ourselves with Christ in our innermost being and, with the Savior in our hearts, we go forward into the new year. For the more distant future too we resolve to be bearers of Christ, to co-operate in the redemption by bringing the Savior to many of our brothers and sisters, to make Him shine out for them, above all by the example we give of a truly Christian life.

THE FEAST OF THE EPIPHANY

The Godhead of Christ Rises Resplendent in His Church

THE feast of January 6 is often called the feast of the Three Kings. The Epiphany is the second great feast of the Christmas cycle of feasts.

It has an oriental stamp, being based on the Eastern concept of the entry of a king into his capital city. The people of those days believed that divinity resided in their prince. It was an "apparition of God," or, as the Greeks called it, epiphany. And that which the heathen peoples attributed in fancy to their ruler became reality with Christ. The Son of God, in human form, enters His city. The liturgy calls it Jerusalem, meaning the Church.

The feast has a monumental character. With the appearance of the Son of God on earth, Jerusalem (the Church) becomes wondrously bright, while, all around, darkness covers the rest of the peoples (the unredeemed part of mankind). But even these, attracted by the bright light (star), begin to gather round, with the "Three Kings" at their head. All mankind is invited into the Church.

*   *   *

Just as, of old, the Three Wise Men from the East brought to the people of Jerusalem the tidings of the newborn King, so today they bring to all Christians the same good tidings of great joy. At the *Introit* of the Mass they call out to us: "Behold the Lord, the ruler, is come, and a kingdom is in his hand."

And so, with the Three Kings, at the beginning of the Mass we bow down before God, the Ruler; and, in the joyful *Gloria,* we pay Him homage once more: "We praise thee, we bless thee, we adore thee!"

The *Collect* draws a striking comparison between the Three Kings and ourselves: Led by the star, they came to the Child in the manger and were permitted to see Him face to face; led by the star of the faith we have been brought to Christ in the Church, that we may adore Him as true God. We ask that one day our faith may find its full realization in the contemplation of God in heaven, in all His glory, face to face.

Particularly charming today are the poetical strains of the *Lesson,* taken from the prophet Isaias. He presents Jerusalem — by which we must still understand the Catholic Church — as a city of light, set in the full majesty of God. Already the *Collect* has softly sounded this truly Christmas note of light; now it bursts forth in all its fullness and splendor. In a vision the prophet sees the Lord of the Messianic kingdom, that is to say, Christ, drawing near to His city. The city is illuminated, reflecting back the light of God, while, all around, darkness covers the earth. And, drawn by this bright light, the peoples begin to gather from all sides, with gifts in their hands, that henceforth they may walk in the divine light. "Be enlightened, O Jerusalem . . . the glory of the Lord is risen upon thee . . . the Gentiles shall walk in thy light . . . thy heart shall wonder and be enlarged." Here we see the Church of Christ of all ages. It is the light set in the beacon, sending forth its rays of truth and sanctity over the whole world, penetrating the darkness of sin and error. Christ, the God-King, lives again in His Church and in it prolongs unceasingly His work of redemption. That is His "appearing," His Epiphany, through all the ages of human history since He came into the world. "He that followeth me, walketh not in darkness, but shall have the light of life" (Jn. 8:12).

Of classic quality, like the whole of the liturgy of today's Mass, is the *Gradual*, as an answer to the Lesson and a preparation for the *Gospel*. It forms in fact a bridge between the two. "Reflectively the *Gradual* re-echoes the two main thoughts of the Lesson: light and gifts. And the *Alleluia* verse throws into relief the main phrase of the *Gospel* which embraces the same two thoughts: light and gifts" (Parsch).

That which Isaias saw seven hundred years before the coming of Christ the *Gospel* now narrates as a reality that has actually come to pass: Led by the gleaming star the first worshipers leave the darkness of paganism to come to Christ the King. Since then countless millions of men have followed them, ourselves included. The star that leads us to the Church of Christ, and there holds us fast, is the holy Faith, the shining, animating, beneficent grace of the Lord, that guides us through darkness and need and raging storm. Today we renew our baptismal vows. By baptism we were admitted into the Holy Church, into "the house in which we find the child with Mary, His mother." Yes, His mother too. "What God has joined together, let no man put asunder." In the Catholic Church, Mary occupies a central position, after and next to Christ.

The Three Kings, as the *Offertory hymn* relates, brought their gifts to Christ the King. We too, through the sacrament of baptism, are of the race of kings, are children of God. And as a sign that we have devoted ourselves with all our soul to Christ our King we too offer Him our gifts. The gold of our love and fidelity. "Take away my liberty, my understanding and my will. . . . Give me only Thy love, and I am rich." We offer the incense of our prayers. "Let my prayer be directed as incense in thy sight" (Ps. 140:2). And we offer the divine Child the myrrh of our little crosses and sufferings. For love of Him we accept them in entire submission to God's holy will.

And the Holy Child shows us that He is not to be outdone in generosity; for, at the *Consecration*, Christ appears on the altar in reality and truth: an epiphany veiled in mystery. More than that, He offers Himself for us to His heavenly Father as Victim. As the *Secret* of the Mass expresses it: "Look down graciously, O Lord, we beseech thee, upon the offerings of thy Church; by which are not now offered gold, frankincense, and myrrh; but he who is signified by those offerings is immolated and received, Jesus Christ thy Son our Lord."

At the *Communion hymn* Mary offers her Child to us, not only to adore but even to be the food of our souls. Then, filled with joy, we leave the House of God, and as we go on our way, outside into the world, we keep singing in our hearts: "We have seen his star" and have adored Him.

FEAST OF THE HOLY FAMILY

The Christian Family

WITH the feast of the Epiphany, the mystery of Christmas is regarded by the liturgy of the Church as having come to a close. Today we see the Savior before us as a boy of twelve years old, subject to Mary and Joseph in Nazareth, and we celebrate in the Feast of the Holy Family the ending of the childhood of Jesus.

There is something extremely attractive in the thought that the eternal Son of God was willing to spend so long a time growing up in the circle of a family. It is His way of affirming the great importance of family life for the whole of human society: as families are, so is the whole of society. The liturgy of today's Mass is easily understood and needs no lengthy explanation: The Holy Family is presented to us as the model for every Christian family.

*   *   *

Right at the outset, to get the atmosphere so to speak, let us look into the house at Nazareth. What a charming picture! Jesus, Mary and Joseph have been called the earthly Trinity. There we see them, three persons with but one heart and soul. They love one another with true devotion, and have their delight in being together. "The father of the just rejoiceth greatly. . . . Let thy mother be joyful. . . . How lovely are thy tabernacles, O Lord of hosts! My soul longeth and fainteth for the courts of the Lord" (*Introit*). Since that time devout souls have meditated with special predilection and in holy rapture on the obscure life of Jesus in Nazareth. Even as a picture of a fine Christian family it is something truly beautiful.

Charmed by the beauty of this scene we turn, in the *Collect*, to the divine Child, with the prayer: "O Lord Jesus Christ, who, becoming subject to Mary and Joseph, didst hallow home life by singular virtues; by their help grant that we (for our own families) may be taught by the example of thy holy family and have fellowship with it for evermore."

And now the *Epistle* tells us of those virtues of which the Holy Family affords us an example to be followed by our own families: compassion, benignity, humility, modesty, patience. What loving compassion must not Mary have felt for Joseph when she saw him toiling to provide for the family! What a fullness of benignity, radiating from the divine Child and uniting the happy parents to one another in tender love for their Child! Joseph was filled with humility and modesty toward Jesus and His mother, as was Mary, for her part, toward Joseph. Filled with humility too, the Child concealed His godhead so that He might show in a completely natural way His deep human love. Never an impatient word from one to the other! And thus, the Apostle tells us, should it be in every Christian family: "Bearing with one another and forgiving one another. . . . But above all these things have charity, which is the bond of perfection . . . in psalms, hymns and spiritual canticles, singing in grace in your hearts to God. All whatsoever you do in word or in work do all in the name of the Lord Jesus Christ! Would that we could have the happiness of gazing for a moment, in a spiritual transport so to speak, into the little house in Bethlehem and seeing the Holy Family at their prayers and at their hymns! How we would wish that such a vision might last forever.

The *Gradual* well expresses this yearning: "One thing I have asked . . . to dwell in the house of the Lord all the days of my life." And at the *Alleluia* we turn again to the Child Jesus: "Verily thou art a hidden king, the God of Israel, the Savior."

The *Gospel* then gives further examples of the virtues of the Holy Family. Together they make the long journey up to Jerusalem to pray and offer sacrifice. This is the churchgoing of the whole family, and we may be sure that at home in Nazareth they went together every Sabbath to the synagogue. What a beautiful sight it is, in our own day too, to see father and mother and children set out together for the church and there receive Holy Communion at the table of the Lord! It strengthens most powerfully that common bond of supernatural love that, in the *Gospel,* we see exemplified in the Holy Family: when Jesus, unnoticed, stays behind alone in the temple and His father and mother for three whole days seek Him "sorrowing," as Mary so poignantly puts it. What an affecting picture of love! And then Jesus goes back with them to Nazareth — and is "subject to them." The incarnate Son of God sets the example of obedience, notwithstanding that Mary and Joseph were so much less than He! Mary, too, stands high above Joseph in holiness and in her dignity as Mother of God, but nevertheless she obeys him as head of the family. Joseph in his humility recognizes that he is the least in holiness, but since God has placed him in command he sees it as the will of God that he should issue orders and directions. What a magnificent example! In the Christian family too, and even in a religious community, the head is not always the most holy, but that has nothing to do with the matter. The subordinates must still obey, since the head, as such, is the representative of God. How splendid it would be for mankind if all the families of the whole world were modeled on the family of Nazareth!

The liturgy provides all of us with the necessary strength, for, at the *Consecration,* He who for thirty years led an obscure life in the family at Nazareth comes down to us and offers Himself as Victim for us to the Father in heaven. And at the *Communion hymn,* with the same unimaginable condescension, He comes into our hearts, as formerly He was subject to His poor parents. Reminded of this in the *Postcommunion* we pray to the Savior: "Let us, whom thou refreshest by thy heavenly sacraments, O Lord, ever follow the example of thy holy family; so that at the hour of our death thy glorious Virgin Mother and blessed Joseph may be near us and we may be found worthy to be received by thee into eternal dwellings."

SECOND SUNDAY AFTER THE EPIPHANY

Our Spiritual Betrothal to Christ

THE two great feasts of Christmas and the Epiphany are now past. The six following Sundays are called "Sundays after the Epiphany" and constitute at first an echo of the Christmas Season and then a transition into the season of Lent.

Today, the Second Sunday after the Epiphany, is still closely connected with the feast of the Epiphany of our Lord, for on January 6 we celebrated (in the Divine Office) three mysteries, each signalizing an epiphany, a revelation of the Godhead of Jesus: (1) The adoration of the Three Wise Men; (2) The baptism of Jesus in the Jordan; (3) The marriage feast at Cana, where Jesus worked His first miracle, thereby proving Himself to be God. On the feast itself the first of these events was celebrated, and on the octave day, the second. The present Sunday raises the third miraculous event to the level of a feast of its own, for behind it there lies veiled a mystery that transcends the marriage feast at Cana: today, now at the Holy Sacrifice of the Mass, the Church — therefore all of us, as the bride of Christ — celebrates her betrothal to Him.

❉   ❉   ❉

Accordingly all the hymns of today's Mass strike a note of jubilation and exultation and are veritable bridal songs, commencing with the *Introit*. At our entrance into the church Christ is already there waiting to celebrate His marriage with our soul. Filled with awe and submissive love, we greet our divine Spouse: "Let all the earth adore thee, O God, and sing to thee: let it sing a psalm to thy name, O thou most High! Shout with joy to God, all the earth, sing ye a psalm to his name!" With the same enthusiasm we then sing the *Gloria*, which for the most part is addressed to Christ, the Bridegroom of our soul.

For our marriage with Christ we must put on a wedding garment, and, in the *Epistle*, Paul tells us what this should look like, in other words how we should show our faith and love for Christ. First, by the conscientious discharge of the duties of our calling: "Brethren: we have gifts differing according to the grace that has been given us, such as prophecy, to be used according to the proportion of faith, or ministry, in ministering; or he who teaches, in teaching; . . . he who presides, with carefulness; he who shows mercy with cheerfulness." The Apostle selects only a few examples, but whatever our calling may be we must practice it conscientiously, in obedience to God, who is the giver of all offices and callings. It does not matter what calling we have; what matters is that in exercising it we shall be faithful and diligent. As a second requisite Paul then names brotherly love: "Let love be without dissimulation. . . . Being of one mind one towards another." Indeed, that is the chief commandment of Jesus, our Spouse: "Love one another, as I have loved you."

And how has God loved us? The *Gradual* tells us how: "The Lord sent his word [His only-begotten Son], and healed them, and delivered them out of their destruction. Let the mercies of the Lord give glory to him. . . . Alleluia. Praise ye the Lord, all his angels, praise ye him all his hosts."

The *Gospel* tells us of the marriage feast at Cana, when Jesus, performing His first miracle, changed water into wine. But this is merely a sign, a picture of a much more wonderful mystery, namely the great marriage of the incarnate Son of God with mankind. What happened nineteen hundred years ago at Cana happens today in a much more exalted reality, at this moment in the Mass. Here, Christ is the Bridegroom and we, His Church, are the bride. He enters into the closest union with us when He gives His divine life to our soul. He takes possession of our soul and of all our thoughts and actions, and gives us in return all that is His: His godhead, His manhood that bled for us, His prayer, His merits. He makes us sharers in His divine life. A solemn deed of joint ownership is drawn up between Bridegroom and bride.

In the *Offertory hymn* we rejoice at this unmerited love and favor: "Shout with joy to God, all the earth. . . . Hear, all ye who fear God, and I will tell you what great things he hath done for my soul. Alleluia!"

At the *Consecration* we assist at a far greater miracle than that of Cana. There, water was changed into wine, but here, just as truly, bread is changed into the Body of Jesus and wine into the

Blood of Jesus, and at the Holy Communion we are admitted to partake of them. Marveling, we say with the chief steward to Jesus our Bridegroom: "Thou hast kept the good wine until now" (*Communion hymn*). Until now, that is to say, until the eucharistic marriage feast. "At what other feast has a banquet ever been given at which the guests, instead of bread, were served with the body of the bridegroom? . . . From His side that was pierced with the lance He fills His chalice with the holy blood and offers it to us" (Jacob von Batna, a Syrian poet of the fifth century). We should be inebriated, as it were, by this precious wine; our tongues should glow with love for our heavenly Bridegroom long after we have left the precincts of the church. As the multitude said of the Apostles at Pentecost on beholding their rapture at the coming of the Holy Spirit: "These men are full of new wine" (Acts 2:13); so too should men be able to say of us on beholding our deep love for Christ and His kingdom when we are wedded with our divine Spouse each day in the Holy Mass.

THIRD SUNDAY AFTER THE EPIPHANY

"Be Thou Made Clean!"

WITH the Third Sunday after the Epiphany the association of the liturgy of the Mass with the Christmas cycle ceases altogether. If Easter should fall early, the Sundays after the Epiphany that are passed over (from the Third onward as the occasion may require) are fitted in between the Twenty-third and Twenty-fourth Sundays after Pentecost. The *Gospels* of these Sundays are an arbitrary selection from the miracles and teachings of Jesus without any regard to chronological order. But as they all deal with a manifestation of the divine power and the grandeur of the Savior — that is, an "epiphany" as God — they have a feature in common that justifies the description "Sunday after the Epiphany." To this extent they have a relationship with the Feast of the Epiphany, January 6.

Furthermore, the psalms are common to these Sundays, the

hymns at the *Introit, Gradual, Offertory* and *Communion* being the same for each Sunday. They celebrate one and the same theme: the greatness and majesty of Christ as God as "manifested" in the *Gospel* of each particular Sunday. To that extent therefore they have now and again a character of their own. In the *Introit* we pray: "Adore God, all ye his angels. Sion heard and was glad, and the daughters of Juda rejoiced. The Lord hath reigned."

❋   ❋   ❋

The basic thought of today's Mass is taken from the *Gospel*, which tells of the healing of a leper. Jesus makes him clean. So today we come to the Mass deeply penetrated with the thought that we too, more or less, are lepers, unclean in our soul. That would be the case, most of all, if someone were to assist at Mass in a state of mortal sin. But even such a one need not lose heart, still less stay away. Just as the leper accosted the Savior, despite the protests of the Pharisees, in a consuming desire to be made clean, so too should the sinner pluck up courage and place his trust in the mercy of God, who may perhaps through this very Mass grant him the grace of sincere conversion, and so make him clean. And whoever is at present free from mortal sin, but has committed such sins in the past, can bring them into today's Sacrifice as though he were still burdened with them. But we are certainly not all of us completely free from venial sins and numerous failings and imperfections, and therefore we are lepers in the all-pure eyes of God. "Who shall ascend into the mountain of the Lord (to offer sacrifice)?" asks the Psalmist (Ps. 23:3), and answers: "The innocent in hands, and clean of heart." If that held good for Jewish sacrifice in the temple, how much more must it hold good for the Holy Sacrifice of the Mass! And how much more again for those who go to Holy Communion and receive the Purest of the pure into their hearts! How does it happen then that so many, despite frequent Communion, do not make more progress? Because they do not sedulously cultivate purity of heart; because, perhaps, they make nothing of quite deliberate venial sins; because in their speech and their actions, they offend against neighborly charity and are so addicted to many venial sins that they have no desire to give them up. That is not how it should be with us today, now, at this moment, at Mass!

At the *Confiteor* we acknowledge in sincere humility the uncleanness, the leprosy, of our souls, and at the *Kyrie eleison* we cry out from the depths of our hearts to the Triune God to have mercy on us. And, in the same spirit, at the *Collect* we implore: "Almighty and everlasting God, mercifully look upon our infirmity, and stretch forth the right hand of thy majesty for our protection." For Jesus cured even the leper by stretching forth His hand.

In the *Epistle* Paul refers especially to one sin which, unfortunately, is common even among Christians, and which covers the soul as with leprosy: aversion, or even hatred, toward our enemies. But if we are to do the will of Jesus we must love our enemies, even those who have offended us, or done us grave wrong, or persecuted us, or sought to injure us. The Apostle enjoins on us: "Revenge not yourselves, but give place unto wrath. . . . But if thy enemy be hungry, give him to eat; if he thirst, give him to drink." How few Christians really do that! They do not return good for evil, thus wiping it out through charity. They are well content if they conquer themselves sufficiently not to do or wish their enemy any harm, but they cannot find it in their hearts to do him good. And how is it with ourselves?

The *Gradual* is as it were a transition toward the *Gospel,* where Christ Himself appears before us to teach us by His word and example. Jubilantly we welcome Him: "Alleluia! The Lord hath reigned, let the earth rejoice: let the many islands be glad!"

In the *Gospel* we see Jesus as the great miracle-worker. A poor leper falls down before Him, saying: "Lord, if thou wilt, thou canst make me clean." And when Jesus sees his utter misery and his still greater trust He answers: "I will; be thou made clean." And forthwith the body that had been covered with corruption and sores became clean and restored to vigorous health. That was done by the right hand of the Savior which touched the sick man as He spoke the words: "Be thou made clean!"

Filled with awe we now sing the *Offertory hymn* in unison with the healed man: "The right hand of the Lord hath wrought strength . . . I shall not die, but live, and shall declare the works of the Lord."

The same all-powerful and merciful Savior then "appears" on the altar at the *Consecration.* Let us ask Him today with perfect confidence: "Lord, if thou wilt, thou canst make my soul clean."

He will do it, for He is offering Himself now to the Father in atonement for our sins and to obtain for us the strength to avoid sin in future. So, to us too, He now speaks the words: "Be thou made clean!"

And then we advance to the communion rail, our minds filled with the thought of the leper and the centurion (in today's *Gospel*). With the leper we implore Jesus: "Make me clean!" With the centurion we acknowledge: You can heal us without coming into our hearts. Do it we beseech you, before you come, so that we may receive You with a pure heart. "Lord, I am not worthy that thou shouldst enter under my roof; but only say the word — and my soul shall be healed." Say only the miracle words: Be thou made clean — and my soul is made clean.

In the *Communion hymn* we read: "They all wondered at these things, that came from the mouth of God." This wonderment of the multitude has to do in the first place with the exalted teaching and miraculous works of Jesus. In choosing these words for the *Communion hymn* the Church wishes to convey that — more even than at the miracles of Jesus at that time — we must wonder at the mystical miracle that Jesus now performs at Mass: At the words of the priest He descends from heaven on to the altar, re-enacts the sacrifice of the cross, and, full of love, unites Himself with our soul in the sacrificial banquet. Truly, anyone who has deep faith must tremble to the roots of his being at the infinite omnipotence and goodness of Jesus, day after day, at every Sacrifice of the Mass.

FOURTH SUNDAY AFTER THE EPIPHANY

"And There Came a Great Calm"

THE *Gospel* of today paints us a charming picture: Out on the sea the boat of the Apostles moves gently on; all around is stillness and night, and the stars shine down on the Son of Man who lies sleeping in the stern. Suddenly the scene changes. A great tempest sweeps down from the mountains and lashes the sea to fury. The little boat is tossed to and fro like a nutshell, the waves pour in on all sides and almost swamp it. The Apostles are terror-stricken and helpless, but Jesus sleeps on and they dare not wake Him. But finally their will to live masters all other feelings; they awaken the Savior and call out with one voice: "Lord, save us, we perish!" Jesus wakes, and hears the reproach that is implied in their appeal. Heedless of the storm, He gently answers their reproach: "O ye of little faith!" Only then does He bid the wind and the waves: Be still! And scarcely are the words spoken when, on the instant, there comes a great calm. Normally it would take hours for a raging sea to subside and for the lashing waves to be appeased. But wind and waves at once obey the command of Jesus: not a breath of air is to be felt, the sea is like a mirror, and on it the little boat rides at ease. "And there came a great calm," as the Gospel so felicitously puts it. That was a prodigious epiphany, a flashing forth, a manifestation of the godhead of Jesus. "What manner of man is this, for the wind and the sea obey him?" asked the men, wondering.

The Savior sometimes preaches not only with words but also with deeds, and this miracle on the sea of Galilee has a symbolical meaning. We are all embarked on our little ship of life, each by himself, out on the sea of the world. Jesus is with us too, for in baptism He came on board our frail bark. Normally we go quite peacefully on our way. But now and then a mighty storm blows up and shakes our little boat, and throws it hither and thither so that we begin to lose heart. One such storm is the raging of the passions. After perhaps a long spell of calm, all of a sudden you are assailed by thoughts and desires, altogether against your will. They threaten to capsize your little boat, to throw you into mortal sin. But as long as you do not consent, there is no question of any sin. Jesus is there with you in your little boat. But you must implore Him: "Lord, save me, or I perish!" The same thing holds for religious doubts, for spiritual dryness and the rest. Another time it is mental or bodily sufferings that are whipped up to a storm. The man who has not spent hours in which he was almost at the point of despair does not know life. Even if, at such moments, Jesus seems to be indifferent to your necessity, and does not wish to be awakened — do not despond: O you of little faith! Call to Him again: Lord, save me, let me not perish — and there will come, to you too, a great calm.

Mindful of our own necessity, but also remembering that at this moment, while we are attending Mass and going to Holy Communion, countless numbers of our fellow creatures are in danger of making a wreck of their lives, let us at the *Kyrie eleison* implore for them with all our hearts the mercy of God. And at the *Collect* let us entreat Him: "O God, who knowest how great are the perils that beset us . . . grant that what we suffer for our sins we may overcome by thy help!"

The *Epistle* lists a number of violent passions, in particular adultery, murder, theft, calumny. But it reserves a very special warning for sins against charity. And certainly we need the warning, for we are often roused to bitter thoughts and feelings against our neighbor which can easily run to provocative words and even worse. Our ego is all too ready to invade the rights of others, and will not even stop short of anger and hatred. But he who daily receives Jesus into his heart in Holy Communion will, by His grace, be able to overcome all uncharitable thoughts and words and actions: "And there came a great calm."

From the example of such Christians, the unbelievers and heathens, so numerous even in our regions, will then be made to see that Christ gives the strength to live in neighborly charity, that He really rules in our soul, and calms the storms of passion. "The gentiles shall fear thy name, O Lord. . . . Alleluia! The Lord hath reigned" (*Gradual*). "The right hand of the Lord hath wrought strength . . . I shall not die, but live, and shall declare the works of the Lord" (*Offertory*). And the more we succeed in living a sinless life, the more must we thank God and praise Him, for to Him alone this success is due.

Since we know that of our own strength we cannot hope to surmount the many storms of life we turn to the Savior, who now comes to us in the Holy Sacrifice of the Mass. We beg Him to come once more at the *Communion* into our little bark, that He may command all the winds and storms that may perhaps arise in the course of this very day. Thus will the holy quiet of the peace of God dwell in our hearts and fill us with wonder at the power of His grace. "They all wondered at these things which came from the mouth of God" (*Communion hymn*).

(The Fifth and Sixth Sundays after the Epiphany will be found at page 164 ff., following on the Twenty-third Sunday after Pentecost.)

SEPTUAGESIMA SUNDAY

"Go You Into My Vineyard!"

THE entire ecclesiastical year is divided into two cycles of feasts: the short Christmas cycle from the First Sunday in Advent to the last Sunday after the Epiphany, and the great Easter cycle from Septuagesima Sunday to the First Sunday in Advent. So today we enter a new sector of the ecclesiastical year. The name Septuagesima itself indicates this, for it means "the seventieth day," namely, before Easter. The season of Lent, beginning with Ash Wednesday, constitutes the immediate preparation for Easter, and the three Sundays preceding Ash Wednesday (Septuagesima, Sexagesima, Quinquagesima — roughly seventy, sixty, and fifty days, respectively, before Easter) constitute the pre-Lenten season; they are the remote preparation for Easter and the immediate preparation for Lent.

The pre-Lenten season that begins today has much in common with the season of Lent proper and already takes on something of its penitential character. The color of the altars and of the priestly vestments is violet; and the joyful *Gloria* and the jubilant *Alleluia* are not heard. Instead of the *Alleluia* after the Epistle, we now say the often quite overpowering prayer of repentance, the Tract (even on feast days of Saints); and at the end of the Mass the *Ite missa est* is said. The *Alleluia* was, in early times, essentially the Resurrection hymn of the Christians, and therefore it has to be omitted in the period of preparation for Easter, both in the Mass and in the Office. We said it for the last time yesterday, at the end of the Vespers of the Saturday before Septuagesima. There, "as if to ease the pain of separation," it is sung twice at the *Benedicamus Domino,* and twice repeated by the answering choir — a truly charming touch of the liturgy. At Easter the *Alleluia* will ring out again as "a new canticle," as an expression of the joyful spirit of Easter.

❖   ❖   ❖

We come now to Septuagesima Sunday itself. In the early Church on this day the adult candidates for baptism were selected, that is to say, those who were to receive the sacrament of baptism at Easter and so were to be resurrected with Christ. Up to that time all such candidates had to undergo an intensive preparation under the guidance of the Church. For us who were baptized as children this period should be a preparation for the Easter renewal of baptismal grace. And so today (in the Gospel) the call of Christ goes out to all mankind: "Go you into my vineyard!" It is a call to a great decision: All of you, attach yourselves to Christ, fight at His side against all that is evil in and around you, withdraw with Him from the world in order to receive with Him the laurel of victory of the Resurrection and Transfiguration. For us who have already for years striven to answer the call it means: strain yourselves to advance still further in perfect union with Christ, to become from year to year ever more deeply absorbed in Him. That is the spirit in which the texts of today's Mass are to be understood.

At the *Introit* we call to mind our human frailty and the many sins we have committed during our life, for self-knowledge is the first step toward improvement. Conversion, the cleansing of the soul — and that is the great task of the period of preparation for Easter — must begin with the recognition that we have need to improve. But we remember also, and include in our prayers, those poor sinners who close their ears to the call of Christ to conversion, who, ensnared in the misery of sin, are spiritually dead. In particular we think of our unfortunate brothers and sisters who at this time of Carnival wantonly give themselves up to sin, and our hearts are wrung with the lamentation: "The moaning of death surrounded me, the sorrows of hell enveloped me. In my distress, I called upon the Lord, and from his holy temple he heard my voice."

In atonement for our sins and those of our fellow creatures, whom in our charity we feel to be one with us, we pray in the *Collect:* "Graciously hear the prayers of thy people; that we who are justly afflicted for our sins may for the glory of thy name be mercifully delivered."

The *Epistle* rings out like a trumpet call that summons our soul to battle against all the evil propensities of our fallen human nature. Therefore abstain from all things. In moving words Paul presents himself as an example of mortification and of the spirit of repentance: "I so fight, not as one beating the air; but I chastise my body, and bring it into subjection, lest perhaps . . . I myself should become a castaway." Even this great Apostle knows well the danger of being led astray by sin. And how he puts to shame those many Christians who frivolously expose themselves to the danger of sin by indiscriminate frequentation of the movies and theater and the reading of unwholesome books, and have no thought for mortification or penance! The second part of the Epistle gravely warns us that the fact that we have been baptized and call ourselves Christians offers no sure guarantee of salvation, no more than did mere membership of the Jewish race. We must labor and struggle and do penance. Truly these are rousing words. It behooves us now to wake from the deathlike sleep of winter. No more winter ease! On to the work of spring! The divine Work-giver has need of us once more to work in His vineyard.

In the *Gradual* we trustingly pray for strength to face this heavy toil: "Thou art a helper in due time. . . . Arise, O Lord, let not man [the man in us] prevail." There follows, in the *Tract*, the contrite yet confident prayer of the sinner: "Out of the depths I have cried to thee. . . ."

As Paul summoned us to fight in the arena, so Christ, in the *Gospel*, summons us to work: "Go you also into my vineyard!" Especially you who still are standing outside, in the midst of the sin of the world, be converted to Me and come into My vineyard. And you who are already living in a state of grace, see that you work still more zealously for your sanctification and for the salvation of sinners. Why stand you there idle! Enter more fully into the enchanted world of the Holy Faith and the love of God, so that with each ecclesiastical year you may advance by the path of penance to the glory of the everlasting Easter in heaven.

We are resolved courageously to answer the call of the Lord, for Christ alone is our happiness. "It is good to praise the Lord, and to sing to thy name, O Most High" (*Offertory hymn*).

Our courage and confidence reach their peak at the Communion, when the Lord of the vineyard comes into our hearts and gives us new strength in our onward striving and our struggle for sanctity. He lets His face to shine upon us, and lets us not be confounded (*Communion hymn*).

SEXAGESIMA SUNDAY

"A Sower Went Out to Sow His Seed"

LAST Sunday summoned us to fight in God's arena, to work in the vineyard of Christ. In the liturgy of today's Mass Christ urgently exhorts us to work at the cultivation of our soul. The picture fits in well with the approach of spring, when the farmer will be scattering the seed over his fields. Two thousand years ago Christ scattered the seed of His divine teachings over the field of the earth, and still goes on tirelessly and unceasingly sowing the seed of His grace in the soul of each one of us. And what has been the result? Only a minority of mankind are Christians. And, of the Christians, the majority do not live up to their Christian Faith. As for ourselves: how hard we often find it to obey the promptings of grace!

And so, at the *Introit* of today's Mass, our soul cries out to Christ: "Arise, why sleepest thou, O Lord . . . and forgettest our trouble: Our belly hath cleaved to the earth." By the material part of our human nature, which we share with the brute creation, we are enslaved to earthly things. Our body, with its many evil impulses, drags us down and makes it difficult for our soul to soar to God and things divine. And yet we know that Christ can help us, and will. So, full of trust we call out to Him: "O Lord, help us and deliver us!" We have heard — "our fathers have declared to us" — how by Your works You have lovingly raised up many who lay prostrate on the ground, and have made of them great saints. Thus Your all-powerful grace transformed Saul, the persecutor of Christians, into the greatest missionary of all time. So can You also transform us. *Christe eleison!*

In Rome today's Station-ceremony takes place in the Church of St. Paul. Therefore in the *Collect* we ask for his intercession: "O God, who seest that we put not our trust in anything that we do of ourselves; mercifully grant that by the protection of the Apostle of the Gentiles we may be defended against all adversity!" This is the only Sunday Collect that makes reference to a saint.

As Paul is presented in the *Collect* as intercessor, so in the *Epistle* he is presented to us as a pattern. In his soul the grace that Christ had scattered bore fruit a hundredfold. Not only did he labor in the fields of the Lord; in the course of his apostolic journeying he also suffered: "in prisons more frequently, in stripes above measure, in deaths often." A reminder that for Christ and His kingdom we too, in the coming season of Lent, should offer up sacrifices and sufferings and works of penance. As a reward for his self-denying work Paul was overwhelmed with extraordinary graces, and it was given to him to enjoy in mystical visions almost the happiness of heaven. Nevertheless he still remained a man, subject to temptation, and feeling in his body the thorn of the flesh. He too could moan, as we have just done in the *Introit:* "My body hath cleaved to the earth," "who will deliver me from the misery of this life?" He answers: the helping grace of Christ is enough. Are we of the same mind? If the seed of divine grace is to grow in us and bear fruit, then, as with Paul, the plough of self-conquest and suffering must be put to our soil, and the ungodly impulses in us must be broken up and overturned. More than ever if God is to bless our soul with grace as superabundantly as He did the soul of Paul. And the seed itself must first die, for only then can it come to life. Thus in our very debility is revealed the power of Christ. "Senseless man, that which thou sowest is not quickened, except it die first" (1 Cor. 15:36). And this is doubly true if, fired with apostolic zeal, one aims not only at saving oneself but also at saving others: "Unless the grain of wheat falling into the ground die, itself remaineth alone. But if it die, it bringeth forth much fruit" (Jn. 12:24).

Paul was the Apostle of the Gentiles. With him therefore let us pray in the *Gradual:* "Let the gentiles know that thou alone art the Most High over all the earth." But how many there are that refuse to hear the Word of God and that reject the seed of the Gospel. Therefore God often sends heavy days of punishment, such as we lived, for example, in World War II, when the bombs fell from the skies and we went in constant fear of our lives: "Thou hast moved the earth, O Lord, and hast troubled it. . . . That thy elect may be delivered."

Let us take earnestly to heart the parable that, in the *Gospel*, Jesus now puts before us and explains. Christ is the divine Sower and our soul is the ploughed land. Already at our baptism He sowed the seed of divine life in our soul through sanctifying grace. Then came confirmation and our First Communion. And since then: how often have we received the sacraments, especially Holy Communion! How many godly inspirations, how many urgings and promptings to good — all of them pure seeds of divine grace! And where are the fruits? How much good seed have we not choked with our indifference, our passions, our evil inclinations, our absorption in earthly not to say worldly affairs and preoccupations!

Let us make solemn resolutions for the future and, in the *Offertory hymn,* pray God that He may Himself protect His precious seed in us, that He may watch over it and bring it to fruition. "Perfect thou my goings in thy paths, that my footsteps be not moved . . . show forth thy wonderful mercies. . . ."

Christ Himself once spoke the words: "A seed cannot bring forth fruit, unless first [in the darkness of the earth] it die." He Himself is the divine seed who offered His life on the cross so that, planted in the souls of men, it might bring them divine life. Now, at the *Consecration,* He renews this death. He is not only the Sower, but also the Seed. In the *Communion,* as the eucharistic Seed, He plants Himself in the soil of our soul. With joy therefore let us approach the altar, the table of the Lord: "I will go in to the altar of God, to God who giveth joy to my youth." Even the old can say this prayer, for, though their body may wither away, their soul, from Communion to Communion, becomes ever more beautiful and radiant until the day when they win the reward of eternal youth in heaven.

QUINQUAGESIMA SUNDAY

"Lord, That I May See!"

WE NOW stand directly at the threshold of Lent, and today's Mass is fully attuned to that season. The candidates for baptism at Easter have been selected. In the early Church baptism was called "illumination" from the fact that it brings to man the light of faith. Christ becomes his leader; without Him man walks in the darkness of death and sin. Hence we are told in today's *Gospel* of the healing of a blind man. We can imagine the profound impression made by this gospel story on the assembled candidates, filled with interior yearning for illumination through baptism. The Gospel also records a second event: Jesus announces the beginning of His passion and death. "The Son of Man now goes up to Jerusalem. There He shall be delivered to the gentiles, scourged and put to death; and the third day he shall rise again." The words are clear enough, and yet the Evangelist adds that the Apostles "understood none of these things, understood not the things that were said." On one occasion Peter even tried to talk the Lord out of the idea of the passion! Even he was spiritually blind, like the other Apostles, in what concerned the great plan of Jesus to redeem mankind by His suffering on the cross.

Appropriately, as if to console us who often cannot understand the true meaning of suffering in our lives and wish to have none of it, the Station-Mass in Rome on this day takes place at the tomb of St. Peter. Particularly in these last days before the season of Lent mankind would seem to become afflicted with blindness, plunging into sinful pleasures of all kinds. Jesus says: I am going up to my passion; and men reply: we are going off to our sinful pleasures. Unfortunates, they do not see that they are standing on the brink of hell. Let us make special mention of these poor souls in our prayers at the altar. But we ourselves are often just as blind. We allow ourselves to be captivated by the things of this world, we are all too prone to act from purely natural motives, and often give no thought to the supernatural, the eternal. Perhaps the reproach of Holy Scripture fits us: "Thou sayest: 'I am rich [in supernatural merits, in virtues] . . . and have need of nothing,' Thou fool, thou knowest not that thou art poor and blind and naked" (Apoc. 3:17). The greatest saints, in their humility, held themselves to be the greatest of sinners.

*   *   *

And so let us approach the altar today in humble consciousness of our blindness and poverty. Let us place ourselves in imagination with the blind beggar of the Gospel at the wayside, where Jesus — now, in the Holy Sacrifice, at the Consecration — passes by. At the outset of the Mass, at the *Introit*, we pray: "Be thou unto me, O

God, protector; for thou art my strength and thou wilt lead me [the blind]!" Christ have mercy on us! In the *Collect* we go on to ask: "Graciously hear our prayers . . . guard us from all adversity!" What Paul says to us today in the *Epistle* on the subject of charity is one of the most beautiful passages of all his Epistles. Would that when we read it the grace of God might remove the cataract from our eyes, that we might see! Above all, that we might realize how much we fail in love of our neighbor. But also that we might learn to see the need that exists in our immediate surroundings and, so far as we can, set about relieving it. How grand a place the earth would be if all men, or at any rate all Christians, did that! Finally, one last kind of blindness: a too great readiness to overlook our own failings altogether, or to take too lenient a view of them. We are, of course, very quick to notice the failings of others, especially when they irritate us, and quite likely they appear graver in our eyes than in the eyes of God. Hence the reproof of Jesus: "Thou hypocrite! Why seest thou the mote that is in thy brother's eye; and seest not the beam that is in thy own eye." Let us earnestly pray: "Lord, that I may see!" Help me to put into practice the words of the Epistle: "Charity beareth all things."

The *Gradual* and the *Tract* are a hymn of praise to the Savior who now approaches in the Gospel, ready to heal us of our spiritual blindness, as He has indeed in many respects already healed us of it, so that the sinful pleasures of the world are no longer a peril for us. So must the poor blind man of the Gospel have given praise to Jesus when his sight was restored and he was able to behold the beauty of the world in Spring: "Thou art the God that alone dost wonders. . . . Sing joyfully to God, all the earth . . . we are his people, and the sheep of his pasture."

Then, in the *Gospel,* when Jesus says: "Behold, we go up to Jerusalem [now in the season of Lent], to suffer for you," let us answer: We shall go with You, we shall suffer with You — in spirit by meditation, and in fact by doing many acts of mortification in the Lenten season. Let us today decide in advance what we shall do for Lent. Unfortunately there are many Christians who in their blindness are ignorant of the very word *mortification.*

In His passage today over the earth, Jesus comes at the *Consecration* also to us who are spiritually blind, and at the *Communion* visits each one of us individually. And so from the depths of our soul we pray to Him: "Lord, that I may see!" Let the scales fall from my eyes and deliver me from all self-deception, even if it should bring the painful realization that I am wretched in Thy sight. Let me in future walk always in Thy light. If we pray thus sincerely to the Savior while He is in our hearts, there will be fulfilled in us too the promise of the *Communion hymn:* "The Lord gave them their desire; they were not defrauded of that which they craved."

THE SEASON OF LENT

WHAT must we do in the season of Lent in order to live it in the spirit of the Church? What is the ultimate significance of this important part of the ecclesiastical year? The liturgy of Lent, and especially of the Lenten Masses, is imbued with three main thoughts. (1) The passion of Jesus. In the first period of Lent, it is true, we are directly concerned only with the struggle of Jesus (and of Christians) against the powers of darkness, though this finally develops into the passion and death. From Passion Sunday onward the passion itself stands in the foreground. (2) The baptismal motif. In the early days of Christendom, when it was mainly adults that were won over to the Church and subsequently, through baptism, admitted to membership, a spiritual instruction for the candidates for baptism was held each day at the Mass, accompanied by the rite of exorcism and other ceremonies. Reminders of these pratices are still to be found in the Lenten Masses of today, in particular on every Monday, Wednesday, and Friday of the week. For us who were baptized as children the season of Lent ought to be a renewal of the baptismal spirit, a strengthening and development to the utmost limit of the grace of this sacrament. Then we shall be ready on Easter night, with lighted candle in hand, to join in the ceremony of the renewal of baptismal vows. (3) Penance. In the olden times, even well into the Middle Ages, those Christians who, after baptism, had committed grave offenses had to do public penance during the whole season of Lent. On Ash Wednesday they received, with the ashes, the garment of repentance, and on a Maundy Thursday, not necessarily the one next following, they were once more received into the community of Christians and admitted thenceforth to the Sacrifice of the Mass and Holy Communion, from which they had up to then been excluded. Let us, on Ash Wednesday, take our place in the ranks of the penitents as, filled with sorrow for our sins, we receive the blessed ashes. In the same spirit let us all through the Lenten season do penance and practice self-denial more than at any other time of the year; let us be more zealous and thorough in the performance of the duties of our calling, and especially let us exercise a certain moderation in the use of food and drink. How otherwise could we join with an easy conscience in the prayers of the Church, where all through the season of Lent the need for fasting, in the strictest sense of the term, is constantly impressed upon us? Many of the Masses of Lent, in particular the Thursday Masses, are a lesson in the true spirit of repentance.

The Station-ceremonies are of special importance for a proper understanding of the Lenten Masses. With the Pope at their head, the Christians of Rome assembled in a given church (Assembly-church) and from there marched in procession to another church, where a halt (Station) was made and the Holy Sacrifice celebrated; for that reason this second church was called the Station-church. On the first Sunday of Lent it was the Lateran Basilica, which is dedicated to St. John the Baptist. That was a very happy choice, for in this church, dedicated to the Baptist, the candidates for baptism were due to be baptized on the coming Easter night. The choice of church for the Station had a great influence on the composition of the texts for the relevant liturgy of the Mass. It was only during the season of Lent that all the faithful of Rome came together in this way in the same church. All in a body, the faithful, the penitents and the neophytes went in procession through the streets of the city, singing and praying. "The fervor of each served to animate the others and the new-found rapture of the neophytes made for the edification of all" (Parsch).

The season of Lent is the holy springtime of the Church (*ver sacrum*) and the dawning of the coming Easter day. New — supernatural — life is to burgeon in this holy springtide. That is true not only for those who are to be baptized at Easter but also for us who were baptized as infants. For it is not new shoots alone that come to life in the spring; the old growth takes on a new verdure and life starts afresh the whole evolutionary cycle from the beginning. Thus for us too Easter becomes in truth a baptismal feast, and it is precisely our penance and our meditation on the passion of Jesus that are the chief nourishment of this new life. The forty days of Lent were for the early Christians what parish missions and retreats are for us today — days of spiritual re-birth in Christ.

FIRST SUNDAY OF LENT

Tempted by the Devil

ONE might at first blush be inclined to regard the story of today's Gospel as outside the realm of possibility: Jesus, the Most Holy, the God-Man, tempted by the devil, in the clutches so to speak of Satan, who even takes Him by force up into a mountain and sets Him upon the pinnacle of the temple! Three times he tempted Him: to the pleasures of the flesh (in the wider sense), when he seeks to titillate His palate, that is to say to arouse in Him a sensual longing for food; then to the pleasures of the eye (covetousness), when he entices Him with the vision of the glory of ruling over a great and beautiful kingdom and promises to give it to Him; and finally, to the pomp of life (ambition), when he bids Him cast Himself down from the pinnacle of the temple so that He may appear to the people below in the temple square as a being descended from heaven, and that they may wonderingly fall down and adore Him as the lovingly awaited Messias. Jesus overcame these temptations by prayer (words of Sacred Scripture).

"The pupil is not above the master." And so, like Jesus, we too are tempted in some way or other almost every day. The devil sets to work on the threefold evil craving that has grown out of our fallen nature: at one moment he tempts us to sensuality and the pleasures of the flesh, at another to greed and covetousness, and again to pride and arrogance toward our fellow men. We must counter his attack with love of poverty, chastity, and obedience. Members of religious orders actually bind themselves to these things by a solemn vow. Satan could only tempt the Savior exteriorly, but with us he can get within and lure both our bodies and our imaginations into sin. Our free will alone he cannot directly touch so long as we do not deliberately yield to the temptation. "The devil is like a hound on the leash, who can make a great deal of noise and bare his ugly teeth, but cannot bite or harm us if we do not ourselves go over to him" (Augustine).

Resistance to temptation is the main theme of today's Mass. We pray and offer sacrifice that we may be given strength not to succumb to the temptations of the devil. At baptism we renounced the devil; today at the beginning of the season of baptismal renewal, we confirm that renunciation. The first condition of a worthy observance of the season of Lent is indeed to live without sin. In the Office for today Pope Leo I says: "The body is profitably deprived of food only when the soul is kept back from sin." Even the fasting itself is a protection against the attacks of the devil, for it takes our thoughts away from our own person and even from those now present with us at the Mass, and makes us think rather of the countless thousands outside the Church who perhaps today, at this very moment, are being tempted by the devil with special severity. We pray with perfect confidence because the goodness of Jesus has made available to us so many powerful aids against temptation: prayer, the Holy Mass and Communion, our guardian angel.

Straightway, in the *Introit* we hear the voice of God speaking to us: "He shall call upon me [in temptation], and I will answer him. . . ." At the *Kyrie eleison* we implore the help of the Trinity for the hour of our temptation.

At the *Collect* we pray especially for strength to be able to resist temptations against our Lenten resolutions, that all through these forty days we may truly lead a life of self-denial and good works: "O God, who dost purify thy Church by the yearly fast of Lent; grant to thy household that what we strive to obtain from thee by abstinence, we may secure by good works."

We firmly resolve — it is the least that we can do in the way of penance — faithfully to carry out the injunctions of the *Epistle*, especially during the Lenten season: to give scandal to no one by bad example, to practice patience, to lead a chaste life, to do kindness to our neighbor. To the worldly-minded we may appear "as dying and behold, we live, . . . as sorrowful yet always rejoicing, as needy yet enriching many, as having nothing and possessing all things." For our whole happiness is locked up in Christ, our Lord. In other words, Paul enjoins on us love of simplicity and poverty becoming modesty, humble devotion to duty and obedience.

Gradual and *Tract:* The fatherly love of God has posted an angel at the side of each one of us to help us to ward off the temptations of the devil, as God Himself tells us in Psalm 90. Let us therefore recite this entire Psalm in perfect trust. The other canticles of the Mass, too, are all taken from the same Psalm. How fine a touch in the liturgy of the Church is here revealed! In his temptation of Jesus, Satan misused a phrase from Psalm 90 ("God hath given his angels charge over thee, to keep thee in all thy ways," therefore cast thyself down from the pinnacle of the temple) and sought to incite Jesus to make a sinful trial of God's trust. Let us, for our part, recite the Psalm in genuine trust that God will help us in the hour of temptation.

At the *Consecration* Jesus immolates Himself for us, that we may obtain strength to resist all the temptations of Satan and of our own nature, especially for this day.

In the *Communion hymn* He unites Himself with us ("under his wings thou shalt trust: his truth shall be thy shield") against the attacks of the devil.

SECOND SUNDAY OF LENT

Strive After Transfiguration

THE great Raphael has painted with wonderful mastery the scene of today's Gospel, the Transfiguration of Jesus on Mount Thabor. The more to heighten the contrast with the transfigured form of the Savior he depicts in the lower half of the picture the casting out of the evil spirit from a boy, which in fact took place immediately after the scene on Thabor. What a contrast it is! Below, deep gloom, the despairing father of the poor child whose body is convulsed by Satan — above, the bright form of Jesus, radiant as the sun.

But long before the famous Italian painter, the Church, inspired by the divine artistry of the Holy Spirit, had painted a similar picture in the texts of the Mass of the Second Sunday in Lent. Sad and distressing are the prayers and Lesson in the first part of the Mass. Prostrate at the steps of the altar the people acknowledge their miserable sinfulness to the whole Court of Heaven, poised invisibly above the altar. We are still wandering through the night of our earthly life. Originally this Mass was celebrated on the Vigil night from the Saturday to the Sunday. On all sides we are beset by the powers of darkness: Satan, our own appetites, a world that is utterly sunk in sin, and we gaze into an abyss of distress and misery. In the *Introit* we cry out to God: "Remember, O Lord, thy compassions and thy mercies, which are from the beginning, lest at any time our enemies rule over us: deliver us, O God of Israel, from all our tribulations!" Lord, have mercy on us! Christ, have mercy on us! Lord, have mercy on us! Thus we call down the mercy of God upon our wretchedness.

And then, how deeply affecting are the words of the *Collect:* "O God, who seest that we are wholly without strength, keep us both inwardly and outwardly, that we may be defended in body from all adversities, and cleansed in mind from evil thoughts!" God will surely hearken to so truly humble a prayer, rising as it does from the depths of the heart and breathing such quiet confidence. And we may be sure that we shall have the support of the Mother of God, the mediatrix of all graces, for the Station-church of this day is the Marian church of St. Mary in Domnica.

In the *Epistle* too (from the First Epistle to the Thessalonians) gloomy colors are here and there laid on, though some rays of light can already be seen breaking through. Reference is made to fornication, profanation of marriage, and defrauding our fellow men in business. Sternly, Paul warns us: "The Lord is the avenger of all these things, . . . God has not called us to uncleanness, but unto sanctification. . . . For this is the will of God, your sanctification." By constant struggle we must attain to our spiritual transfiguration.

As in the Epistle, so too in the *Gradual* and the *Tract*, the Raphaelesque chiaroscuro is dominant. We strive here below after our transfiguration, our sanctification, but we know too that God is good and that He will give the right dispositions to those who pray to Him for them. Therefore, confident of victory, we go on to pray: "Give glory to the Lord, for he is good. His mercy endureth for ever. . . . Remember us, O Lord, in the favor of our people: visit us with thy salvation!"

At the *Gospel* our loving Savior replies: Yes, I shall hear your humble prayer, and one day I shall grant that you too shall be transfigured as I have been this day. My own Transfiguration shall bring it about in you.

And now, in the second part of the Mass, the scene brightens. At the *Offertory* we sing: "I will meditate on thy commandments, which I have loved exceedingly; and I will lift up my hands to thy commandments which I have loved." The yearning for our own transfiguration makes every sacrifice easy. Nothing is too great for our love.

At the *Consecration*, that which the Gospel has announced becomes living reality. The altar is Mount Thabor and the transfigured Savior appears, even though it be under the veil of the sacrament. And God the Father, looking down with pleasure on our sacrifice, says: "This is my beloved Son, in whom I am well pleased." In deep reverence, we adore.

In the *Communion hymn* the Savior unites Himself with our soul, intensifies in it the light of sanctifying grace, and imparts to it something of the purity of His white garment and His radiant countenance. It is a foretaste of the promise of Jesus (Mt. 13:43): "Then shall the just shine as the sun in the kingdom of their Father!"

THIRD SUNDAY OF LENT

Baptismal Casting Out

IF WE wish to understand the texts of the Lenten Masses we must see them in their historical setting. At that time, in the early centuries of Christianity, every Lenten Mass was preceded by a procession. The faithful assembled at a prearranged point in Rome, and then, praying and chanting the *Kyrie eleison,* they went in procession through the streets to a given church, where they halted and assisted at Mass. This was called the Station-church. As far as possible, out of the many churches in Rome, a different church was chosen for each day. On the Third Sunday in Lent it was the Church of St. Lawrence Outside the Walls. Let us picture in our minds the long procession as it moves toward the church: in front, the candidates for baptism (catechumens), behind them the penitents in their garments of sackcloth, then the faithful, both men and women, and finally the clergy with the pope. As they enter the Station-church we hear the strains of the *Kyrie eleison,* and then of the *Introit,* so-called because it is sung at the entry into the church.

Both for the penitents (Christians who after baptism had sinned openly and grievously and now had to do strict penance in this season of Lent) and also for the catechumens, these forty days had been a time of purification, of penance, of preparation for the union with Christ on Easter Sunday in baptism and Communion. Humble and contrite they turned their gaze on Christ. And so today's *Introit* was directed also toward Christ, whose image shone down on them from the apse of the Station-church: "My eyes are ever toward the Lord, for he shall pluck my feet out of the snare [of the devil]. Look thou upon me, and have mercy on me, for I am alone and poor."

The *Collect* is in the same strain: "Almighty God, regard the desires of the humble . . . be our defence!" Defense against what? Against Satan and sin. For it is sin that keeps man from Christ: sin, brought about by the devil in league with the lusts and allurements of the world around. On the Third Sunday of Lent it was the practice to submit the candidates for baptism to a ceremonial casting out of the devil (exorcism). Before baptism man is, if not actually possessed by the devil, at least to a very great extent subject to his power. To this day even the little children, when they are brought to the church to be baptized, have at the outset to undergo a casting out of the devil. That is why the Gospel of today treats of a casting out of the devil by Christ.

Assembled there in the House of God stand the catechumens, most of them already adult men and women, who are still heathens and therefore still particularly exposed to the power of the flesh

and the devil, but who nevertheless are consumed with longing
for Christ and His kingdom. Hence the admonition of the Church
in the *Epistle* (taken from the Epistle to the Ephesians): "But
fornication, and all uncleanness, or covetousness, let it not so much
as be named among you [much less happen], as becometh saints
[when you shall be baptized]. . . . Let no man deceive you with
vain words. For because of these things cometh the anger of God
upon the children of unbelief." Cast down by these stern words
the catechumens, at the *Gradual* and in the *Tract,* pray in answer:
"Arise, O Lord. . . . Let the Gentiles be judged in thy sight. . . .
To thee have I lifted up my eyes."

What the first part of the *Gospel* now relates, the casting out of
a devil by Christ, happens today to the catechumens, who are
delivered of the evil spirit in preparation for their baptism. And
then comes the grave warning of the second part of the Gospel:
even though now the devil has been driven from your soul, and,
in his place, One stronger than he, Christ, has entered it through
baptism, you are still not safe from Satan and sin. For he returns,
and finding it cleansed by baptism, takes with him seven other
spirits to conquer it again. This warning holds good also for our
day. In the sacrament of baptism Christ took the place of Satan
in our soul. But alas, if we nevertheless relapse into mortal sin
Satan will use every device to make us fall away from our faith
in Christ. And then we are faced with the words of St. Paul: "It is
impossible for those who were once illuminated [in Baptism], and
have tasted also the heavenly gift [Holy Communion], and were
made partakers of the Holy Ghost [Confirmation], and are fallen
away, to be renewed again to penance" (Hebr. 6:4). Clearly, what
St. Paul means is that it is extremely difficult for such as these to
find their way back to Christ.

The archdevil, even for Christians, is the spirit of impurity. It
is this sin of ours that brought on the Savior His frightful sufferings
at the pillar. His garment has been torn from His body; unceasingly
the blows come crashing down; His blood spurts forth until the
pillar is red. Now all is still, and only the drip of His blood on the
ground is to be heard. Unconscious, Jesus sinks to the earth, and
lies in His own blood. O sin of impurity, what thou hast done!
"If upon some wantoning couple or other, with their lewd laughter,
the door were suddenly to open, and the Lord Jesus Christ were

to enter, looking as He looked after the scourging at the pillar, and fix these light-hearted sinners with His gaze — how their jests would die upon their lips, how they would be seized with horror and would fly from each other's arms!" (Stiegele.)

Hence we renew our resolution faithfully to observe the Commandments of God: "The justices of the Lord are right, rejoicing the heart and his judgments are sweeter than honey, for thy servant keepeth them" (*Offertory*). And at the *Communion hymn* we unite ourselves once more with Christ, the great Conqueror of Satan and our passions. We are resolved never again to lose Him from our hearts. With Him alone do we find happiness. "The sparrow hath found herself a house . . ." (*Communion hymn*).

FOURTH SUNDAY OF LENT

Holy Joy

WHAT a contrast between today's texts and those of the preceding Sundays! Up to now we have heard of temptation by the devil, to the dread point of being possessed by him; of sin and sinful pleasures. Today the Holy Mass opens with a joyful *Laetare*, and all the other texts too breathe holy joy. Today, instead of the somber violet, the priest wears rose-colored vestments, and the organ, which has not been heard since the beginning of Lent, can once more send forth its peals.

Whence this change? Why the rejoicing? The early Church rejoiced at the great hosts of candidates for baptism who on Easter night were to become her children — it was a holy maternal joy. The Church of our day rejoices at the many good deeds that still today are performed during the season of Lent, and especially at the good Easter Confessions. And if we ourselves have faithfully carried out the resolutions that we made on Ash Wednesday for these forty days, that too, gives us a reason for rejoicing and courage to persevere in them right through to Easter Sunday.

Today is a kind of pre-Easter. Just as on the Third Sunday of

Advent (*Gaudete*) we experienced, in childlike anticipation, something of the joy of Christmas, so it is today with the coming of Easter. Penance and suffering are not goals in themselves but only stages on our journey to our goal. Just as, for the Savior, the bleak darkness of Good Friday was followed by the glory of the morning of the Resurrection, so too for us the everlasting joy of heaven awaits us when our life on earth is over. "O happy atonements," cried St. Peter of Alcantara after his death, when he appeared to St. Teresa of Avila, "O happy atonements, that have won for me such splendor." This eternal joy is the blossoming of penance done during this earthly life; but, even in this world, the men of repentance have the greater share of joy. Finally, the Church rejoices today at the resurgence of nature, in which it sees a symbol of Christ's resurrection and our own. For we are now in early spring. On this day in Rome the first roses were brought to the church, presented to one another by Christians for that purpose. Today too, Laetare Sunday, the Pope blesses a golden rose and offers it as a gift to some distinguished personage. Truly, from the *Introit* right to the end, there is a look of spring about the liturgy of today's Mass.

❈   ❈   ❈

Anyone who examines the texts of today's Laetare-Sunday Mass will immediately notice that they have one thing in common: they all deal with the various sources of holy joy.

The first source of joy for Christians is their membership in the Church. Just as, in the Old Testament, the Jewish faithful at Easter time made joyful pilgrimage to the Temple in Jerusalem, so in Rome on this day the early Christians marched out to the so-called Church of the Cross in Jerusalem, and there assisted at the Station-Mass. And this church, in turn, was for them a symbol of the heavenly Jerusalem to which we are all making our pilgrimage together. This community feeling itself is a true source of joy that finds expression in the *Introit:* "Rejoice, O Jerusalem! And come together all you who love her. Rejoice with joy, exult, and be filled from the breasts of your consolation." The Church is to us as a mother, who has given us birth in baptism to be children of God, and who nourishes us constantly in sanctity.

First place in this nourishment — and here lies a further source of joy — goes to the grace of interior illumination and sweet comfort that God sends us in prayer and at times in the liturgical services. For this we pray in the *Collect:* "Grant that we may be relieved by the consolation of thy grace," and have our courage renewed to face the hardships of life "which are the punishment of our misdeeds."

In the *Epistle* Paul presents the Church in the roles of princess and queen. We, her children, are therefore not bondmen, but free. Through sanctifying grace, which we first received in baptism and since then have added to in rich measure, we are children of God and heirs to heaven. That is the very foundation of true joy. He who lives in a state of grace is free from the slavery of Satan, free too from the sins of the flesh, and may even now rejoice, in anticipation, over his reward in heaven: "Brethren, we are the children of promise!" And therefore in the *Gradual,* despite the season of Lent, we reply with a hymn of jubilation: "How I rejoice; we shall go into the house of the Lord [heaven]. . . . As the mountains are round about us, so the Lord is round about his people from henceforth now and for ever."

The *Gospel* refers to a further source of joy, the *Eucharist,* of which the feeding of the multitude with bread was at once the token and the promise. Exactly a year later Jesus transformed bread into His most holy Body, thus fulfilling what He had promised. Hence at the *Offertory* we sing Him a canticle of praise: "Praise the Lord . . . whatsoever he pleased he hath done." Even when, as with the multiplication of the loaves, it required a great miracle; for He is the All-powerful. And now, at the *Consecration,* behold He performs once more a great miracle, providing the bread from heaven, and, by the hands of His apostle of today, the priest, distributing it to the multitude. Not thousands only, but millions, partake today of a bread that is Christ Himself.

And all this is but a foretaste and a pledge of the ineffable, everlasting joy of the Jerusalem of heaven, to which, sustained by this holy food, we are journeying as pilgrims. With eyes uplifted, therefore, we sing our joy in the *Communion hymn:* "Jerusalem built as a city, compact together; thither did the tribes go up, to praise [eternally] thy name, O Lord."

Christ Comes as High Priest to the Altar of Sacrifice in the Bloody Garments of His Passion

Up to today the season of Lent has been devoted mainly to our spiritual purification by prayer, fasting, penance, and overcoming the temptations of the devil. We are now ready, in the last two weeks before Easter, to join in the passion of our Savior, which occupies the central place in the Mass texts of each day. Even in the Preface we see clearly this change of tone. Hitherto the Prefaces during Lent have spoken of the fruits of penance and fasting. From today onward the cross becomes the focal point (of veneration): the salvation of the human race is determined in the cross. "In the cross is salvation!" But why, then, does the Church, on today of all days, decree that the cross shall be veiled on the altars? She withdraws the image of the crucified Savior from our gaze in order that we may the more interiorly meditate on the cross and the passion of Christ and impress them on our soul, so that on Good Friday, when the cross is once more unveiled, the mystery of the passion of our Lord may all the more overwhelm us.

* * *

An artist (Gottwald) has painted for today the following illuminated initial in the Missal: Christ, as priest, clad in gothic vestments, stands before us with arms outstretched, the blood flowing from the five wounds as if He already hung upon the cross. This summarizes admirably the sense of the texts of today's Mass: On Passion Sunday Christ begins His bloody sacrifice, recites, as it were, the prayers at the foot of the altar. Hence the opening words of our customary prayers before the altar come today in the *Introit,* for which reason the psalm "Judica" is omitted from the prayers before the altar today and in all the other ferial Masses right up to Easter. Christ calls upon His Father to judge between Him and the unholy Jewish people who take up stones to attack Him.

"Judge me (*Judica me*), O God, and distinguish my cause from the nation that is not holy!" And then the Savior, as man, implores the heavenly Father to give Him strength to bear His approaching passion. "Send forth thy light and thy truth; that they may bring me unto thy holy hill [of Calvary].

In the *Epistle*, Paul — in the spirit of the illuminated initial just referred to — gives us a picture of Christ as the Priest-victim for our sins. The Apostle enters into a description of the sacrificial rite of the Old Testament in which oxen were slaughtered to make propitiation to God for sin. The priest collected in a bowl the blood of the slaughtered animal and carried it to the innermost part of the temple, into the Holy of holies, to offer it before the face of God as an atonement for sins. In the New Testament, says Paul, Christ is the High Priest and at the same time the Sacrificial Lamb. By His death on the cross He enters the Holy of holies — the veil of the temple is rent at that moment — and appears before the face of the Father, not with other blood but with His own, to offer expiation for the sins of the whole world through one, unique, bloody sacrifice for all ages: a sinless Priest, an unspotted Lamb. "Behold the Lamb of God, who takes away the sins of the world!"

Whilst we meditate on the words of the Apostle we hear, in the *Gradual* and the *Tract*, the moving voice of the Savior raised in lamentation yet full of serene trust in the help of the Father, just as we shall later hear Him pray in the Garden of Olives on the evening before the passion: "Deliver me from my enemies, O Lord, teach me to do thy will [Not my will but thine be done]. . . . Often have they fought against me from my youth [already as Child in the manger, and in Egypt]. Yet they could not prevail over me. . . . The Lord who is just, hath cut the necks of sinners." In the end, through His Resurrection Christ will prevail.

The *Gospel* then tells us of these enmities, and we are made to fear the worst for Jesus, His approaching death. At first His enemies attack Him with angry words and revile Him, the Sinless One, as devil, no less. In answer Jesus points to His eternal birth from the Father, thus proclaiming Himself God: "Before Abraham was made, I am." "They therefore took up stones to cast at him," for in the Old Testament death by stoning was the punishment for blasphemy. But Jesus "went out of the temple." This has also the symbolic meaning that Jesus leaves His faithless, rebellious people to their destruction. The sun of the day of Christ, that "Abraham . . . rejoiced that he might see," sets on the people of the Old Testament, but only to shine out the more gloriously on Easter morning on the Church of the New Testament. The judgment announced in the *Introit* has begun.

Jesus is now ready to offer the bloody sacrifice to the eternal honor of His Father. He prays to Him for strength: "I will confess to thee, O Lord, with my whole heart. Give bountifully to thy servant; I shall live and keep thy words." Truly a hymn of sacrifice!

Once only, and that for all time, did the eternal High Priest, Jesus Christ, consummate His bloody Sacrifice. But countless times, today too, now at this solemn moment, He renews the Sacrifice in an unbloody and mystical manner at the *Consecration* of the Holy Mass. At the *Communion* we receive His flesh and blood as a sacrificial repast, and are reminded in the *Communion hymn:* "This is my body . . . this is the chalice of the new testament . . . do this . . . in memory of me." But this memory must not consist in a mere grateful remembrance of the death of Jesus long ago; it must, for each one of us, become present reality. Today we enter with Christ into the Passiontide, to offer ourselves up and to suffer with Him. We will not let Him suffer alone. We shall win redemption only if we too carry the cross after Him. "Today the Church veils the cross. Is it perhaps that we are no longer worthy to look upon it? . . . Christ took upon Himself the cruel scourging, bore the crown of thorns, carried the heavy cross — and we? We pamper our bodies . . . we are impatient if we are called on to bear for Christ the minutest splinter of His cross" (Benedikt Baur). It is not enough that, filled with exalted thoughts, we now take part in the solemn liturgical ceremonies, and then, once we leave the House of God and return to our daily lives, sullenly turn our back upon the cross. There have been saints who out of love for the suffering Savior have scourged themselves and have even implored Him to send them sufferings, expressly that they might share in His passion. Even though we may not have the courage, or the love, necessary to do these things, at least we can resolve from now on faithfully to observe the fast and to bear with patience the trials that are incidental to life, accepting them in union with the sufferings of Jesus. In this spirit let us enter today upon the season of the passion.

SECOND SUNDAY OF PASSIONTIDE
or PALM SUNDAY

THE magnificent ceremonies of Palm Sunday are a drama in three Acts: In the Assembly-church (St. Silvester's in Rome), which is meant to represent the Garden of Olives, there is the blessing of the palms (Act 1). From there the faithful proceed in procession (Act 2) through the streets of Rome to the Station-church (Lateran). There the Third Act is enacted: the Holy Sacrifice of the Mass. For us, unfortunately, most of the ceremonies have to be compressed into a single church.

Blessing of the Palms

Under the new rite of Palm Sunday the blessing of palms is performed by the priest in full sight of the congregation and facing it. The elaborate blessing of former years and the *Missa sicca* or "Dry Mass" by which it was preceded have now been replaced by a very simple ceremony. The celebrant, in red cope, with attendant ministers vested in red, goes to the table where the palms or other branches have been placed, the choir singing the *Antiphon:* "Hosanna to the Son of David! Blessed is he who comes in the name of the Lord! O King of Israel, hosanna in the highest!" The short prayer of blessing is then said: "Bless these branches of palm (or other tree), Lord, we pray thee, and grant that what thy people this day bodily perform in homage to thee, they may spiritually perfect with the greatest devotion, by gaining a victory over the foe, and ardently loving every work of mercy: through our Lord Jesus Christ, thy Son, who is God, living and reigning with thee in the unity of the Holy Spirit, for ever and ever."

Strictly speaking each member of the congregation at this service should receive the palm from the hand of the priest. If you can do this, then do it with holy reverence and with understanding of the whole ceremony. Whoever receives the palm, which is the badge of martyrdom, from the hand of the priest, declares himself ready to be a witness (martyr) for Christ before the world, and, in particular, to follow the King of Martyrs, if necessary even unto death.

Procession

To enter properly into the spirit of the liturgy we should now go out, the martyr's palm in our hand, on to the streets of the city, and there sing out our exultant hosannas to our Lord, as once on this day His disciples and followers, and especially the children, acclaimed the Savior at His entry into Jerusalem and escorted Him when, mounted on a she-ass, He rode in triumph through the city. Rapturously they greeted Him, waving their palms, as He entered in state into Jerusalem, not to found there an earthly kingdom but to die for us. But by that very fact He won for Himself spiritual dominion over all mankind. As, palm in hand, we walk in procession, it behooves us, in the silence of our hearts, to declare ourselves ready to follow the Savior even unto death, thus gaining for ourselves the glory that is everlasting. That is the significance of the martyr's palm in our hand. In this spirit we acclaim the Savior, who, in the holy cross that is carried at the head of the procession, accompanies us on our way: *"Gloria, laus et honor* — Glory, praise and honor be to thee, Christ, our Redeemer!"

Oh, would that every word that we speak today, every ceremonial act that we perform, really had behind them our whole being, and an entirely dedicated faith! Only thus shall the promise of the last stage of the procession become true, for us too, one day.

Mass

The ceremonies so far have been emblematic, in part, of the past, in part, of the future; looking backward we commemorated the entry of Jesus into Jerusalem, and looking forward we meditated on our journey of life, which ends with our entry into the heavenly Jerusalem. In the third Act of today's drama all this becomes mystical reality. Jesus Himself, with His godhead and manhood, enters the church and re-enacts — though in unbloody form — the purpose of His entry into Jerusalem: His holy passion and death. Every text of this Mass speaks of the passion of Jesus; it is the most sorrowful requiem of the whole year. It is as it were an anticipation of Good Friday, when of course the Holy Sacrifice is not offered. Hence, already today the passion commences and the sufferings of Jesus are portrayed. In particular, the psalms (*Introit, Tract,* etc.), consist altogether of the supplications and lamentations of the Savior in His extreme abandonment.

We have but to surrender ourselves to this mood of the passion of Jesus, and all the texts become clear of themselves. And when, at the *Consecration,* the Savior lies on the altar as the Lamb-Victim, flesh and blood separated from each other in the chalice and the Host, and when, at the *Communion,* He actually comes into our hearts as the eucharistic food, we once more — as we have already done at the procession — declare ourselves ready to go with Him to His passion and death. At baptism (and at Ordination and Religious Profession) we have already promised Him this. It must not be that after the ceremonies are over when we lay aside the palm we lay aside this martyr-spirit as well. It is only then, in our everyday life, that it has to be put to the test. Many people have the pious custom of taking the wisp of palm home with them from the church and attaching it to the crucifix in their homes. There it serves for the whole family as a reminder of the promise they have made at the procession to keep faith with the crucified Savior in their daily lives when He calls them to sacrifice.

MAUNDY THURSDAY

The Last Supper

AT THIS evening's Mass we must carry ourselves in imagination to the room of the Last Supper and take our place among the Apostles. There we see Jesus Himself celebrating the first Mass and personally distributing the first Communion that was ever given. How must the Apostles have been thrilled when their Master raised up the bread and said: "Take ye, and eat: for this is my body." And then the chalice: "Take ye, and drink: for this is my blood which shall be shed." And then He adds: "Do this in memory of me." With that single sentence He established at the same moment and for all time both the Most Holy Sacrament of the Altar and the Priesthood. These are the two great gifts of Jesus on this day. It is as if He had said: What I have now done — transubstantiated the bread and distributed Communion — that also shall you Apostles and your successors do for the faithful; I hereby give you that power.

The Most Holy Eucharist is familiar to us from childhood on. Yet it ought not to become for us an everyday thing, in the sense of ordinary, that one no longer adequately values. Day after day we ought to assist at Mass and receive Holy Communion with the deepest faith and the greatest reverence, and during the day visit the Savior in the tabernacle. These are the three bright jewels of this sublime mystery: Jesus offers Himself up for us, gives Himself to us for food, and dwells at all times among us. How barren and empty our lives would be, had we not this most holy sacrament! When I was doing my Theology in Rome it fell to me to be in attendance for several days on a missionary bishop who had come from Japan. I was able to observe how, at the Consecration, at the Communion, and afterward at his thanksgiving, the cheeks of this man glowed, so deeply was he stirred by the holy mystery. And of St. Aloysius we are told that every time he celebrated Mass his eyes were filled with tears!

We shall never be able fully to comprehend the unfathomable love that the Savior has bequeathed to us in the Sacrament of the Altar. In taking leave of this world — all His utterances at the Last Supper bear the impress of leave-taking — He yet wished to remain with us, with all His faithful, through all the ages. His love finds a way: He instituted this sacrament so that, hidden under the appearance of bread, with His godhead and manhood, He might always be near us. To all His faithful He comes with joy and love, even if the communicant should be only a little old woman who is not able to keep her mind very much on anything any more. That is a truly generous, self-immolating, servile love; and that is what the Savior expressed in the phrases which preceded the institution of this Most Holy Sacrament.

Jesus stands up from the table — the Apostles following Him expectantly with their eyes — throws a towel over His shoulder, takes a basin of water, and kneels down in front of Peter, to wash his feet. The Apostle is taken aback: that his Master, the Eternal Son of God, should wash the feet of him, the simple fisherman! What truly unimaginable condescension, rather what abasement! In many religious communities we come across a variation of this, when the Superior puts on an apron and waits on his subordinates at table. But the condescension of Jesus in the Eucharist is incomparably greater; in His love He wishes to be servant to us all. We too must serve one another in love, after the example of Jesus. "I have given you an example, that you also may do in like manner."

Normally, in each church or oratory only one Mass may be celebrated this evening. At this Mass, the other priests of the parish receive Holy Communion from the hands of the celebrant priest just as the Apostles did at the Last Supper from the hands of Jesus. Thus today we form in the fullest sense one holy community, gathered round the Savior, who offers Himself up for all of us and gives Himself to us for food.

THE LITURGY OF EASTER NIGHT

AT THE start of the ceremonies of Easter night the liturgy leads us out into the darkness of the night. It is the season of early spring. In this *vere beata nox,* at the entrance to the church a fire is kindled, preferably struck from a flint. This fire is now blessed, and from it is lighted the Easter candle which is the symbol of the resurrection: in the darkness of the night Christ went forth from the stone, that is, from the tomb that was cut into the rock. He is the Light of the World that shines in the darkness of our life. Through the redemption we became one with Him in baptism, and His divine life, bright as light, streamed into our souls, so that we became "light of light." That is the significance of the lighting of the other candles from the Easter candle: on the one hand, Christ, the "Light that is the light of men"; on the other, we Christians, the bearers of His light into the darkness of the wicked world like the wise virgins who with burning lamps went forth to meet the bridegroom to join with him in the marriage festival at the midnight hour. The meaning of this symbolism is explained in the words of the Blessing of the Fire: "Grant us, Lord, through this Easter festival, to be so inflamed with heavenly desires, that with pure minds we may arrive at the festival of perpetual light." A procession is now formed to carry the Easter candle into the church, and the candles of the clergy, of the acolytes and all assistants, are lighted from it in the order of their precedence.

By Christ's redemptive death and resurrection the divine light was brought to the dark and sinful world. This now comes to expression in the *Exsultet,* the jubilant hymn of overflowing joy at Easter night and its great mystery. The whole of creation is invited to the Easter rejoicing. All present join in spirit in the hymn, rising to their feet while it is sung and holding the lighted candle in their hand.

This hymn of exultation is now followed by the four *Lessons:* the first tells the story of the creation of all things at the beginning of time. This Lesson is related, as indeed are all four, to the sacrament of baptism which is to be administered this Easter night. What the liturgy means in this: God wonderfully created the world at the beginning of time, but still more wonderful is the work of redemption. By the passion and resurrection of Christ our human nature was lifted out of itself and filled with divine life. The redemption, as Paul says, is a re-birth. And the rest of created nature must co-operate in our redemption, as when, in the Holy Mass, bread and wine are taken and changed into the Body and Blood of Christ for our salvation, and as too, in baptism the water is filled with the Holy Spirit, that mankind may be born again. Just as, at the beginning of creation, the spirit of God floated over the waters, and out of the formless chaos shaped the cosmos, the marvelously ordered world, so on the night of Easter the spirit of God descends on the water in the font, from which the baptized will come forth as re-created, newborn beings, filled with divine life. As Creator, Christ is the Lord of nature, and as Redeemer, the Lord of grace and of the supernatural, the Lord of all ages and of all men. That is why the Easter candle is inscribed with the words: "Christ yesterday and today — beginning and end — alpha and omega — His are all ages, His the centuries — His are the glory and the Kingdom — through all the aeons of eternity." For the reading of the Lessons we remain seated, but at the end of each of them all stand up. The priest says *"Oremus,"* then *"Flectamus genua."* In this the new rite re-introduces an old custom. All, priest and people alike, kneel down on both knees and remain so for a short while in prayer. Then the priest himself (and not the server) gives the word to rise: **Levate!** In all this the repose of our Lord in the tomb and His resurrection — holding promise also of our own — are intended to be symbolized.

The second Lesson tells of the passage of the Israelites through the Red Sea. The chosen people were saved, while Pharaoh and the Egyptians — symbolizing sin — were covered by the waters. The whole story is of course another reference to baptism, in which our old self, with all its guilt and punishment, is buried in the water, and a new self, modeled after Christ, emerges from the water grave.

The third Lesson refers to the glorious fruits of the redemption and baptism, as can be readily understood from the texts themselves.

In the fourth Lesson the Church, through Moses, calls on us Christians to lead a holy life and to be faithful to the commandments of God.

After the Lessons comes the Litany of the Saints, which, under a new decree (in contrast with earlier practice), is divided into two parts, between which is intercalated the blessing of the baptismal water, the administration of the sacrament of baptism, and the renewal of baptismal vows. For the candidates as well as for those who have already been baptized we invoke the intercession of all the saints, that they may obtain for us the grace to lead truly Christian lives, as befits baptized persons, children of the Light, members of Christ. Each of us will here think in particular of the saints whose names we were given at baptism. After the blessing of the baptismal font and the baptism, if there should be an infant or an adult to be baptized, there follows for all the renewal of baptismal vows: it may be many, many years since we were baptized, but we are now called upon to live our baptism over again and to receive it once more in spirit on this most holy Easter night. All stand up to hear the priest deliver a short allocution taken from St. Augustine; then the priest puts a number of questions to be answered by the entire congregation: We renounce the devil — We believe in God, the Father Almighty . . . Our Father. . . . Finally the priest sprinkles the congregation with the holy water, and some appropriate hymn is sung.

At the end of the renewal of baptismal vows we kneel once more while the second part of the Litany of the Saints is sung as a prelude to the Easter High Mass. The prayers before the altar are omitted altogether, as was the case at the time of the original Easter night ceremony. While the choir sing the *Kyrie* the priest proceeds to incense the altar. On this day the *Gloria* rings out with a special solemnity for in the earliest times it was only at Easter that it was allowed to be sung at all in the Mass. For the rest, the Mass of Easter night is a Mass for the newly baptized. This is made clear particularly in the *Collect:* "O God, preserve in the new progeny of thy family the spirit of adoption which thou hast given; that, renewed in body and mind, they may exhibit in thy sight a pure service." The *Epistle* is an exhortation to the baptized, that, with the transfigured Christ, they may lead a new life. Immediately as it is finished we hear again the joyful notes of the *Alleluia,* last heard on Septuagesima Sunday. In token of jubilation it is sung three times by the priest in a rising voice and repeated by the choir in the same key. The *Gospel* brings us the first news of the Resurrection of Jesus. And then come the high points of the Mass, the *Consecration* and the *Communion.* At the *Consecration* the resurrected Lord appears to us. This is the true feast of the Resurrection: Jesus Himself comes to us in reality, whereas in the popular representations of the resurrection only His picture is placed on the altar. Formerly the laity had to go without Communion during the past two days. That is now no longer the case. Indeed, if they have devoutly followed the glorious ceremonies of Holy Week, then today they are better prepared for their Holy Communion than at any other time of the whole year. Let us, therefore, partake of the Lord as of the Lamb that has been slain for us. Then, as the priest leaves the church, the congregation appropriately sing the hymn "The Lord is risen." And so we celebrate Easter night up to the hour of night when Jesus arose from the dead. On Good Friday, out of love for Him, we sought to share His Passion; today, out of the same love, we seek as it were to assist also at His resurrection.

EASTER SUNDAY

"I Have Risen, Alleluia!"

EASTER is the greatest day of rejoicing of the ecclesiastical year, the "Feast of feasts." Today the heart of the resurrected Savior is filled with ineffable joy, for now is ended the terrible passion by which He has redeemed the world. To all men of all time He has opened the gate of heaven; all they need, in order to be happy forever, is to be of good will. How the heart of Mary also must have overflowed with joy when her Son, miraculously transfigured, stood before her after His resurrection! And what joy and emotion must have filled the Apostles during the whole of that Eastertide! We too wish to taste something of that Easter joy. Just as, since Passion Sunday, we have been lovingly immersed in the suffering of Jesus, so now at Easter we wish to be sharers of His joy.

The Station-church today is St. Mary Major, the greatest of all the Marian churches in Rome. In company with the happy catechumens of Easter night let us turn to the mother of the risen Savior, to her who is our mother also and has procured for us the rich graces of baptism. Let us offer her from our hearts our Easter greeting: "Rejoice, O Queen of Heaven, thy Son is risen!"

How moving is the *Introit* of this festival Mass! Victorious, the risen Christ appears before the Father in heaven and addresses Him lovingly: "I arose, and am still with you, alleluia." It is fitting that the first Easter greeting of the Savior should be for the Father; for it was the Father who had sent Him into the world for our redemption. Out of obedience to Him He had gone to His death; but once His soul is reunited with His body, in a new transfigured life, the first thought of Jesus is for the Father. His morning prayer in the glory of this Easter morning goes out to the Father: "I arose, and am now with you forever, alleluia! Thou hast laid thy hand upon me [led me in my life on earth through darkness to the light for the redemption of mankind], wonderful is thy knowledge, alleluia! Thou hast proved me, thou hast known my sitting down [Mount of Olives, the tomb], and my rising up." We can apply this exactly to ourselves: we too go before the Father in heaven, and the hand of the heavenly Father is stretched out to us in goodness and wisdom even though we may not always take it and may sometimes feel His restraining hand to be a heavy burden. At the end of our life we too shall appear before the Father in heaven and shall say to Him: I arose, and am now with Thee forever; to my eternal happiness, Alleluia! Wise was Thy guiding of my life on earth, Alleluia!

Today we sing once more the joyous *Alleluia*, last heard in the Office for Septuagesima Sunday, two full months ago. It is the outpouring of our Easter rejoicing. The *Gloria*, too, we sing today with special fervor; in early times it was only at Easter that it was sung at all. In it we give praise to the risen Savior as "the lamb, who takes away the sin of the world."

At the *Collect,* in union with Christ, we pray earnestly that the Father may vouchsafe that we too shall win the Easter crown of victory that is eternal life. Christ has opened for us the gate of heaven.

What we have to do, in order that our prayer may be fulfilled, is set forth for us by Paul in the *Epistle.* For him, Christ is "the lamb that went to the slaughter." As we partake of the Lamb today in Holy Communion let us follow the prescription given to the Israelites for the eating of the symbolical paschal lamb on their departure from Egypt: only unleavened bread, baked without yeast, was to be used. "Therefore let us feast [today] not with the leaven of malice and wickedness, but with the unleavened bread of sincerity and truth." At all times and above all things let us seek only God. Just as Christ has now taken up His abode in heaven, so let us make our abode on earth to be also a heavenly abode.

Today, as happens only on the very greatest feasts, there is added, after the Alleluia of the *Gradual,* a *Sequence,* which gives so to speak the reason for our rejoicing and is in the nature of an extension of the Easter *Alleluia verse.* It consists of a short Easter play. We ask Mary Magdalen, who, with two other women, first brought to the disciples of Jesus the news of His resurrection: "What thou sawest, Mary, say, as thou wentest on the way [to the tomb]?" She answers: "I saw the tomb wherein the living one had lain; I saw his glory as he rose again . . ." And the message was clear: He is risen, He is not here. It is an anticipation of what the *Gospel* of today relates in simple narrative form: the fact of the resurrection of Jesus.

In the midst of our rejoicing the *Offertory* introduces a sobering reflection: the resurrection of Jesus is at the same time a judgment on His enemies, on those who will not believe in Him. "The earth trembled, when God arose in judgment." Textually the Scripture says: "And behold there was a great earthquake; For an angel of the Lord descended from heaven, and coming, rolled back the stone [from the tomb of Jesus]. . . . And for fear of him, the guards were struck with terror, and became as dead men" (Mt. 28:2–4). With the resurrection of Christ the triumph of Christianity over the earth was sealed for all time. In belief in Easter lies the great division in the minds of men. Then surely will the earth quake, and His enemies tremble, when the risen Christ comes in the clouds of heaven to deliver judgment on those who have not believed in His resurrection and His divinity.

This judgment is foreshadowed in the destroying angel who on that prefigured Easter night before the exodus from Egypt slaughtered the first-born of the enemy, passing over the houses of the Israelites which were marked with the blood of the lamb. Today, therefore, at the *Communion,* let us sprinkle ourselves with the blood of the true Easter Lamb. Let us take our place with new fervor at the side of Christ and dedicate our whole lives to Him. Here, now, at Mass, we are celebrating the eucharistic feast of Easter.

LOW SUNDAY
(also called WHITE SUNDAY)

Preserve Unspotted Thy Baptismal Robe!

THE great feasts of the ecclesiastical year have an octave, that is to say they are celebrated for a week. Easter, the Feast of all feasts, has a so-called jubilee octave: it is celebrated not merely for seven days but for seven whole weeks. Pentecost, in fact, is the great octave day of Easter. And as Pentecost itself has an octave the Easter season extends to the Saturday after Pentecost. All through this period the joyous Alleluia of Easter is heard with increasing frequency. The *Introit* has two, the *Gradual* has as many as four, and one is added to the *Offertory* and *Communion* hymns. Likewise the festive Gloria, omitted during the whole of Lent, is sung, each day, even in ferial Masses. The Easter Preface continues to be recited, so great and so sustained is the joy of the Church at the resurrection of Jesus, which is also the pledge of our own resurrection.

And whence comes the name *"White Sunday"?* At their baptism
on Holy Saturday the catechumens of the early centuries received
a white robe as a symbol of their baptismal innocence. Just as
Christ, bright as the sun, rose from the darkness of the tomb, so
the baptized, with pure and radiant souls, rose from the baptismal
stream, clad in the festal robe of sanctifying grace. With Christ
they had risen from the dead. During the whole of Easter week
they wore their baptismal robe at the Holy Mass. Then, on yesterday, the Saturday after Easter, they laid aside the white robes at
the end of the Mass. Today, the Sunday of the discarded white
robes, they appeared at the Sacrifice for the first time without the
white garments, in their ordinary clothes. That signified that they
were now perfect Christians. They promised today to remain true
to their baptismal vow even to the death. Appropriately, this took
place in the Church of St. Pancras, who as a boy of fourteen
years sealed his baptismal vow with his blood. True to his example
the newly baptized, who exteriorly had laid aside their white
baptismal robe, were to preserve interiorly their baptismal innocence even unto death: risen forever with Christ from the death
of sin.

*   *   *

In the opening words of the *Introit* of today's Mass, the Church
addresses the newly baptized as newborn babes: As the newborn
child hungers and thirsts for his mother's milk, and, by drinking it,
grows strong and healthy, so must we Christians with hungry longing seek to imbibe the supernatural nourishment of our soul in
frequent Communion. Baptism and Communion are complemen-
tary. How fitting it is that in many countries White Sunday should
be the day for making one's first Holy Communion! Let us think
of our own First Communion today, but let us think also of our
baptism.

The best way to preserve our baptismal grace is by frequent, if
possible daily, Communion. And thus will be fulfilled what we
implore in the *Collect:* "Grant that we who have celebrated the
Easter rites may, through thy bounty, ever cleave to them in our
life." The sons of baptism must arm themselves for their daily life,
and live as risen sons of Christ.

Exceptionally, it is not Paul who speaks to us today in the
Epistle, but John the Apostle. He addresses himself to those who are

"born of God," that is to say, to the baptized. "Whatsoever is born of God overcometh the world; and this is the victory which overcometh the world, our faith. Who is he that overcometh the world, but he that believeth that Jesus is the Son of God?" What a magnificent expression of the triumphant spirit of Easter! There still is today, thank God, no lack of Christians whose belief in Christ as the Son of God, affirmed in baptism, has overflowed in flesh and blood. Everywhere and always they live their lives according to this faith, even when it means facing persecution. Even when suffering comes they are unperturbed, because they know that it comes from God, our Father, whose children we have become by baptism. This faith overcomes the world with all its pleasure and sin. And — John continues — there are three in heaven and three on earth that give testimony of this faith. In heaven, the Father, Son, and Holy Spirit. On earth, "the spirit, the water and the blood." These are the three Easter sacraments that in the early centuries were received one after the other on Easter night: Baptism (water), Confirmation (spirit), and Communion (blood).

The *Gospel* goes on to refer to still a fourth sacrament, which we may also call an Easter sacrament since it was instituted by our Savior on the evening of Easter Sunday when He said to the Apostles: "Whose sins you shall forgive, they are forgiven them." The Savior knew the weakness of human nature, knew that all too many Christians after baptism relapse into sin; and it is for them that He instituted the sacrament of penance. Thomas, who was not present at the time, declared to the other Apostles: "Except . . . I put my hand into His wounds, I will not believe." Eight days later — that is to say today — it was given to him to do so. But Jesus reproved him: "Blessed are they that have not seen, and have believed!"

After we have particularly and joyfully proclaimed in the *Offertory* our faith in the resurrected Christ, He Himself appears among us at the *Consecration*, and at the *Communion* gives Himself to us to eat. We do not see Jesus, and cannot, as Thomas could, place our finger in His wounds. Nevertheless we fall on our knees and, filled with faith, we pray: "My Lord and my God!"

SECOND SUNDAY AFTER EASTER

"I Am the Good Shepherd!"

IN HER ardent love of the Savior the Church sees Him under ever changing forms. In Easter week, for example, as the Easter Lamb who was slain for us and restored to life. Today she presents Him to us as the Good Shepherd. This picture was a favorite one of the first Christians, who, in the days of their bitter persecution, often scrawled it on the walls of the catacombs; it was, so to speak, their Picture-of-the-Sacred-Heart. It filled the lives and the minds of these early Christians.

It is fitting that the Church should particularly place it before our eyes at this season of Easter: by His redeeming death and resurrection — both were celebrated together at Eastertide as a single whole — He proved Himself in the clearest manner possible to be our Good Shepherd; for He gave His life for His sheep, even for those that had strayed. And immediately after His resurrection He sought out all His scattered, frightened sheep, gathered them once more into one flock and gave them in place of Himself a new Shepherd, since He Himself would have to leave them. It is, therefore, a truly Easter picture that the liturgy of today's Mass would imprint upon our hearts. In every part of the Mass we meet with the charming picture of Jesus, the Good Shepherd. It is the Heart-of-Jesus Mass of the ancient Church.

In the *Introit* the mercy and goodness of the Good Shepherd are stressed. With hearts full of gratitude we acclaim Him: "The earth is full of the mercy of the Lord, alleluia! By the word of the Lord the heavens were made." This means by the words spoken by Jesus at Easter: I baptize thee; I strengthen and seal thee with the Holy Spirit; take ye and eat, this is my flesh, my blood; thy sins are forgiven thee — truly sacramental words, transforming, for us Christians, earth into heaven. For we are by each sacrament interiorly united with God, and it is in this union with God that heavenly happiness consists. "Alleluia! Rejoice, O ye just [ye redeemed], praise becometh the upright!"

At the *Collect* we see the Good Shepherd bending down to the

lost sheep that had got entangled in thorns, and, Himself wounded
by the thorns, shedding His blood to set it free. "O God, who in
the humility of thy Son didst raise up the fallen world"; Jesus
takes the poor strayed sheep on His shoulder.

It is appropriate that in the *Epistle* of today it should be Peter
that speaks to us, since he had himself known the forgiving love of
the Good Shepherd and, despite his sins, had been set up as His
successor. He describes the love of the Good Shepherd in His passion and death: "Christ suffered for us . . . who did no sin." In
perfect meekness He bore all His suffering. "When he was reviled,
did not revile; when he suffered he threatened not, but delivered
himself to him [Pilate] that judged him unjustly [to death]; His
own self bore our sins in his body upon the tree . . . by whose stripes
you were healed. For you were as sheep going astray, but you are
now converted [by the sacraments of baptism and penance at
Easter] to the shepherd and bishop of your souls." All men were in
a state of sin. Lovingly the Son of God comes to them as shepherd.
He wards off the wild beasts — hell, sin, death, and Satan — and
snatches the strayed sheep from the claws of the evil one. Then,
having rescued His poor sheep and brought it to safety, He is Himself slaughtered by the wild beasts. No other shepherd does this,
allows himself to be torn to pieces and devoured in place of the
sheep. Jesus alone is *the* Good Shepherd, who actually "gives up
His life."

It is in this guise that He joined the dejected disciples on the road
to Emmaus, instructed them, comforted them and, at the breaking
of bread, allowed Himself to be recognized by them. "I am the
good shepherd; and I know my sheep, and mine know me" — as the
Alleluia verse after the *Epistle* proclaims with joy.

In the *Gospel* Jesus points to two distinguishing marks of the
good shepherd, therein portraying Himself: first, the good shepherd
offers himself for his sheep, even to giving up his life for them.
Jesus did this in His death on the cross. Second, he knows individually each separate sheep entrusted to him, and loves it with
anxious care. The Savior even compares this love of the shepherd
with the love that exists in the bosom of the Trinity between Himself and the Father — "as the Father knows me [with loving under-
standing] and I know the Father." Would that all of us really and
profoundly believed these words of the Good Shepherd! Each one

of us should say to himself: Christ knows me, knows all my weaknesses, but He knows also my good will. He looks after me as if I were the sole object of His care.

Therefore we too, His poor sheep, know the Good Shepherd, that is, love Him with our whole heart. Our first thought on waking in the morning speeds to the Savior in the tabernacle. At our morning offering we flock around the Good Shepherd: "O God, my God, to thee do I watch at break of day; and in thy name I will lift up my hands, alleluia!" [*Offertory hymn.*] This is the voice of the little sheep, its answer to the love of the Good Shepherd as portrayed for us in the two Lessons.

But it did not satisfy the infinite shepherd love of Jesus to offer Himself for us but once. No, at every *Consecration* He renews in a mysterious manner His sacrifice on the cross. When today at the Elevation, the host and the chalice are raised on high, Jesus speaks to us: I give My life to you, lambs of My flock. And His love goes still further. At the *Communion* He does what no other shepherd can do: He gives Himself to His lambs to eat. That is the best pasture He can take us to. In this most intimate union with us is realized in the highest sense the promise of His words: "I know mine, and mine know me" [*Communion hymn*]. It is a knowledge of the most intimate mutual love. O most joyous Easter reality: we are known by the Good Shepherd, and we have known Him! Particularly so in the moments after Holy Communion when Jesus abides in our hearts. Like the disciples at Emmaus we recognize Him "in the breaking of bread."

THIRD SUNDAY AFTER EASTER

Filled With the Joy of Easter in the Midst of Earthly Suffering

TODAY once more, at the *Introit* of the Mass, the risen Savior stands before us as vanquisher of death and hell, and as our Redeemer. We, the redeemed all over the wide earth, summon the whole world to sing Him a song of praise: "Shout with joy to God, all the earth, sing ye a psalm to his name, Alleluia! Give glory in his praise. Alleluia! . . . How terrible are thy works, O Lord [thy redemption and resurrection], and how great is thy strength, that thy enemies lie down before thee!" At the resurrection the guards of the tomb fell as if dead to the ground.

And so today also, as on the previous Sundays after Easter, our spirit is at first carried away by the glorious vision of the Redeemer and the wonderful work of our redemption. But now comes a change. The liturgy of the Easter season moves on and turns our gaze toward the future, and an undertone of woe creeps into our Easter rejoicing. For the Savior Himself announces to us in the *Gospel* that He will not be with us much longer — "because," He says, "I go to the Father." The ascension is drawing near, when Jesus is to leave us behind, alone in the world. Hence the somber thoughts that we find in the remaining texts of today's Mass. But our Easter happiness, our joy over Jesus and our resurrection are nevertheless maintained. In the midst of our earthly suffering we are filled with the gladness of Easter. That is the dominant thought today in the liturgy of the Mass.

In the *Collect,* we ask the Savior once more, before He ascends into heaven, not to let us go astray, but to send down from heaven His strengthening grace, that evermore we may lead Christian lives: "Grant that all who are counted of the Christian faith may cast aside whatever is opposed to that name [of Christian]."

In the *Epistle* Peter brings us a very apt comparison: "Ye [Christians] are pilgrims and strangers" in this world. That is indeed a fact: whoever leads a truly Christian life is bound to feel himself a stranger on this earth. He knows that "we have not here a lasting city."

We carry in our hearts a deep longing for higher things, for the eternal, conscious at all times that we are traveling toward our everlasting home in heaven. And the older we become, the more do we long "to be released, and be with Christ," our risen Savior. Let us, then, not allow ourselves to be held back by the allurements of this world. Let us rather obey the injunction of the Apostle: "Refrain yourselves from carnal desires . . . having your conversation good among the gentiles; that . . . they may . . . behold your good works." Be subject to your superiors and to public authority. "Honor all men; love the brotherhood [your fellow-Christians]."

Clearly, in order to be able to lead such a life, we require help from above. Hence we lift up our eyes to heaven, to our eternal home. There we hear the voices of the angels and saints coming down to us in the Easter *Alleluia:* "Alleluia! The Lord sent redemption to his people [to you]. It behoved Christ to suffer and to rise from the dead; and so to enter into his glory, Alleluia!" The joys of the everlasting Easter in heaven will be ours too, after our days of suffering here below are ended.

The *Gospel,* also, speaks to us today of earthly suffering on the one hand and of our Easter gladness on the other. Our life indeed is very like to that of the Savior, whose thirty-three years — that the Father had allotted to Him for His life on earth — are now spent. And so He says today to the Apostles: "A little while . . . [and then] I go to the Father." His short life of thirty-three years — truly a little while — was rich in privations, struggles, trial, and suffering. But now it is all over, and no one can take His happiness away from Him any more. So is it also with you, says Jesus to His followers: "You shall weep and lament, but the world shall rejoice." Often, things seem to go better for the children of the world; they allow themselves every pleasure and satisfaction, while we renounce all this and lead a life of mortification and self-denial. "But," Jesus continues, "your sorrow shall be turned into joy. . . . I will see you again [in heaven], and your heart shall rejoice, and your joy no man shall take from you."

Yes, that is how it is. Our life too, let it run to sixty years or more, is still but "a little while." St. Teresa of Avila likens it to a short halt at an inn: We go in, have a look around, chat a little with the other travelers, have something to eat — and then we are off again. If only we would use our few years of life with an eye to eternity! Like the Savior, we too meet with much suffering during our stay on earth, perhaps even with contempt and persecution. Our life is a struggle against sin, a real time of trial. Nevertheless we can say with Paul: "as sorrowful, yet always rejoicing" (2 Cor. 6:10). The true Christian is always a man of Easter. Even now we bask in the splendor of the glory to come.

During the "little while" that is still given to us let us travel with courage the sacrificial path of true imitation of Christ, with the song of today's *Offertory* in our hearts: "Praise the Lord, O my soul;

I will sing to my God [even in suffering] as long as I shall be, Alleluia!"

Every day, indeed, at the Holy Mass and *Communion,* the risen Savior comes to us. In strange guise, it is true, as formerly to the disciples at Emmaus. But it is still our Lord that comes to us and gives us strength to live on as men of Easter. And when the time arrives for our last Communion He will come to call for us and will say: "A little while . . . and you shall see me, because I go [with you] to the Father, alleluia! alleluia!"

FOURTH SUNDAY AFTER EASTER

"I Go, to Send You the Comforter"

THE present Sunday, in comparison with those that have gone before, marks a still further step forward. Last Sunday Jesus announced to the Apostles: "I go to the Father." Today He adds: "I go [to send you] the Advocate," the Holy Spirit. And then He describes in detail what works the Holy Spirit will perform on earth. Thus the Mass already becomes a remote preparation for Pentecost.

Truly great were the things the Savior had already given the Apostles in His works of redemption and resurrection. And now, in addition, He promises them today the communication of the Holy Spirit, a new miracle of the inexhaustible goodness of God. Hence we rejoice in the *Introit:* "Sing to the Lord a new canticle, alleluia! For the Lord has done wondrous deeds, alleluia! He has revealed his justice in the sight of the nations, alleluia!"

✿   ✿   ✿

This song of thanks and praise then overflows in the *Collect* into a fervent supplication that God may truly send us the promised Holy Spirit, who is truly the soul of the Church, the spirit of unity which through the bond of love makes us brothers and sisters of Christ: "O God, who makest the faithful [through the Holy Spirit] to be of one mind and will; grant that thy people may love what thou dost command, and desire what thou dost promise; that amidst the changing things of this world our hearts may be set where true joy is found." In heaven, whither the Savior is soon to go before us. "Lift up your hearts," the priest exhorts us at the *Preface,* and all reply: "We have lifted them up unto the Lord!"

The solemn words of the *Epistle,* too, point to the Holy Spirit. "Dearly beloved: . . . every best gift is from above, coming down from the Father of lights." For, on the feast of Pentecost, the Father and Son are to send down the Holy Spirit and His gifts from above. Now we must prepare for His coming by cleansing our hearts of all passions. "Let every man be . . . slow to anger . . . casting away all uncleanness. . . ." This is what the Apostle James enjoins on us today: we must conquer irritableness, impatience, spitefulness, licentiousness. Otherwise the Holy Spirit cannot operate in us.

Then, in the *Gospel,* the Savior Himself tells us of the efficacy of the Holy Spirit in our soul and as a shield against the evil world. "I go to him that sent me. . . . It is expedient for you that I go, for if I go not, the Paraclete [the Comforter, the Holy Spirit] will not come to you." In accordance with God's plan of salvation the Holy Spirit is to come in the place of Jesus to carry on and complete His work of redemption. Therefore the manhood of Jesus must first go forth from this world. The disciples were depending too much upon the physical presence of their beloved Master, and more and more were expecting from Him the setting up of His visible kingdom. So Jesus says to them: It is expedient for you that I depart. Your conception of the kingdom of God must become much more spiritual, much more interior, for the kingdom of God is in fact within you. The Holy Spirit will then become a living force working in your soul, and will lead you to a deeper knowledge of My teaching which you have not yet fully comprehended. For, though the Apostles and disciples had been so long with Jesus they were still far from understanding Him. But when the Holy Spirit descended on them they immediately began to address words of profound wisdom to the people. That was the working of the Holy Spirit in the Apostles, and that is the working of the Holy Spirit in our souls: He brings us to a full understanding of Jesus and inspires us with enthusiasm for Him.

Against the wickedness of the world, too, the Holy Spirit reveals

His efficacy. As Jesus Himself tells us: "He will convict the world of sin, and of justice, and of judgment." First, "of sin," namely that the world does not believe in Christ. That was the great sin of the Jews, that despite the many miracles and the sanctity of Jesus they did not recognize Him, and even nailed Him to the cross. But as soon as the Holy Spirit descends on the Apostles they are able to go forth before the people and give testimony of the resurrection and divinity of Christ, all by the power of the Holy Spirit. Through miracles, worked by the Holy Spirit, they confirm their testimony. Thus did the Holy Spirit convict the Jews of the sinfulness of their lack of faith in not believing in the miracles of God. And it is equally true of the unbelief of later times and of the present day. Second, says Jesus, the Holy Spirit will convict the world "of justice," that is to say, sanctity, since He goes to the Father. How could Jesus go to the Father in heaven if He were really the evildoer that the Jews held Him to be when they condemned Him to death? But when the Holy Spirit comes it is a proof that Jesus is with the Father. Thereby He is established as the All-holy. Holy too, consequently, are His teachings and the Church established by Him and all its doctrines. Finally, the Holy Spirit convicts the world "of judgment." The Jews forced Pilate to condemn Jesus unjustly. But by the Resurrection of Jesus and by the spreading of His kingdom over the earth through the power of the Holy Spirit the world is convicted of the injustice of its judgment. So justice goes forth over the earth, and "the prince of this world is already judged." The world is falsehood and deceit, pleasures of the eye and of the flesh, and the pomp of life.

With full hearts we rejoice at the marvelous power of the Holy Spirit and sing in the *Offertory:* "Shout with joy to God, all the earth, . . . and I will tell you what great things the Lord [through the Holy Spirit] hath done for my soul, Alleluia!"

It may at first glance surprise us that in the *Communion hymn* the liturgy of the Mass should repeat the words of Jesus: "When the Paraclete [the Holy Spirit] . . . shall come, he will convict the world of sin, and of justice, and of judgment." What the Church means is this: At Communion, together with Christ, the Holy Spirit too comes again in a special manner into your hearts. And when later you go from the communion rail out into the world, you must be so filled with the Holy Spirit that you yourselves, each one of you, shall convict the world saying as it were to them: you are wrong, not to believe; in my practical life I am the proof that there is such a thing as earnest striving after holiness. Thus is the world already judged, even before Christ Himself comes in the clouds of heaven to judge the living and the dead.

FIFTH SUNDAY AFTER EASTER

"Ask, and You Shall Receive!"

THE season of Easter, in the narrower sense, is coming to a close; for in five days' time the Savior will ascend into heaven. No wonder, therefore, that in today's liturgy the two thoughts, Easter and Ascension, are blended together.

The *Introit* still is pure rejoicing at the happiness of Easter, at the Resurrection of Jesus, and our own, with Him, in baptism. "Declare the voice of joy, and let it be heard, alleluia! Declare it even to the ends of the earth: the Lord has delivered his people, alleluia, alleluia!" That is our inner happiness at Eastertide: we are delivered from sin, from Satan, and even from death, which comes to us of course, but only to set us free again. We have been redeemed! We are children of God! And so we turn our thoughts to God: "My God and my all!" At the *Collect* we pray to God that we may preserve the spirit of Easter throughout our life and translate it into fact. "Grant that by thy inspiration we may think those things that are right, and do them under thy guidance." Only thus shall we become true and perfect Christians, whose piety shows itself also in our lives. There must be no contradiction between our prayers in the church and our everyday life in the world. Always and everywhere we must be seen to be "risen with Christ," to be dead to all sin, to be true men of Easter.

The same earnest exhortation is addressed to us by the Apostle James in today's *Epistle*. It seizes in fact on the last words of the *Collect* and enlarges on them: "Dearly beloved: Be ye doers of the word, and not hearers only, deceiving your own selves. . . . Not becoming a forgetful hearer but a doer of the work, [this man] shall be blessed in his deed." If we wish to preserve the Easter grace of spiritual resurrection, we must put into practice all the teachings that Jesus expounded to us during His life on earth. The Apostle lays special stress on love of our neighbor in word and deed. "If any man think himself to be religious, not bridling his tongue, this man's religion is vain. Religion clean and undefiled . . . is this: to visit the fatherless and widows in their tribulation, and to keep one's self unspotted from this world." We may notice that at other times too the texts of the Mass, especially the Epistles, are wont to contain exhortations to a virtuous life. Today we have it all in a nutshell: true Faith, and a life in accordance with it — these alone make the perfect Christian.

As if in echo to this solemn Lesson we now sing with glad hearts the Easter *Alleluia*. For we are firmly resolved by God's grace always to live as children of God and to be "doers of the word" as counseled by the Apostle. "Alleluia, Alleluia! Christ is risen, and hath shone upon us whom he redeemed with his blood. Alleluia." Scarcely have the strains of the chant died away when we hear the voice of the Savior in our ear: "I came forth from the Father, and am come into the world; again I leave the world and go to the Father." "And go to the Father" — how sublime are these words, how filled with majestic grandeur!

Thus is struck the second chord of today's Mass: Jesus is about to ascend to the Father in heaven. But, as He immediately assures us in the *Gospel*, He will nevertheless remain in union with us. For He goes only to be our mediator with the Father in heaven, and our advocate. So powerfully does He intercede for us that our prayers in His name are always heard. "Amen, Amen, I say to you, if you ask the Father anything in my name, he will give it to you." But, poor creatures that we are, how weak is our faith! We cannot bring ourselves to take these words literally. And yet they embrace an immensely comforting truth, veritable tidings of great joy. Would that we had more trust in the prayers that we say when we are in a state of grace! When we are united with Christ through grace, the Father loves us as He loves His Son, and grants our every prayer, even though not always in the way that we may wish. For, as we have one (divine) life with Jesus, the heavenly Father hears in our prayer the voice of His Son, and hearkens to us. In view of this promise of Jesus we might well call the present Sunday Petition Sunday. It is an appropriate setting for the three coming Rogation days. In the *Offertory* that now follows we rejoice at these glad tidings of Jesus, that He will hear all our prayers: "Bless the Lord, our God, ye gentiles . . . blessed be the Lord, who hath not turned away my prayer. . . . Alleluia!"

And now in a few moments comes the fulfillment of the promise of Jesus: "I came forth from the Father, and am come into the world," namely down on to the altar at the *Consecration*. And here is fulfilled too that other promise of Jesus: "Where there are two or three gathered together in my name, there am I in the midst of them." Now He joins with us, as our intercessor, in the prayer that He Himself has taught us: "Our Father!" It is a prayer that we should always say with concentration — since every phrase contains a profound thought — and with the conviction that whatsoever we shall ask the Father He will grant us. A moment later, in the *Communion*, the soul of Jesus unites itself with our own; He lives in us and prays in us and with us to the Father. Then He re-ascends into heaven taking with Him all the wishes of our hearts to put them before the Father. And He assures us: "The Father loveth you, because you have loved me." And so, after the Communion, we sing with joyful hearts: "Sing to the Lord, Alleluia! . . . Bless his name . . . from day to day!" Let us treasure the Sacrifice of the Mass beyond all treasures, for in no way and at no time can we so truly pray in the name of Jesus as here. In this liturgical prayer and sacrifice, as nowhere else, we form a great holy community with Jesus and with each other.

ASCENSION DAY

"The Lord Is Ascended With the Sound of Trumpet!"

IT is seldom that a Mass so overflows with joy as on today's feast. Jubilation and exultation are dominant from the beginning to the end.

In the *Introit* we see as in a picture the moment of the ascension of Jesus into heaven. A light cloud has enveloped Him and hides Him from the upturned gaze of the Apostles and disciples. But they do not move from the spot, and keep looking up to heaven, thinking that perhaps the form of the Master will emerge from the cloud once more. Then appear two angels, who say "Ye men of Galilee, why stand you looking up to heaven? [He] shall so come, as you have seen him going into heaven." "Clap your hands, all ye nations, shout unto God with the voice of joy." Again today the Easter Alleluia! For today is brought to completion in heaven the triumph of our Lord which began on earth forty days ago with His resurrection.

We now sing the hymn of joy, the *Gloria*, "Glory be to God in the highest," and today we address it particularly to the Savior as He ascends into heaven and there "sits at the right hand of the Father." Thither, with the Apostles, we turn our gaze as we sing: "We praise thee, we bless thee, we adore thee. Thou only art holy, thou only art Lord, in union with the Father and the Holy Spirit!"

In the *Collect*, it is true, we are made conscious that we ourselves are still wandering on earth, left behind by the Savior. Therefore we pray that at least in spirit we may dwell "in mind of heavenly things," just as the thoughts of Mary, the Mother of God, from this day forward were constantly with her Son in heaven.

In contrast with other feast days, both the *Lesson* and the *Gospel* bring us the news of the mystery of today's feast. It is as if the fact of the Ascension of Jesus into heaven had to be confirmed on all sides as a real event of history. In the *Lesson* we are told, from the Acts of the Apostles, how the Apostles, immediately before His Ascension into Heaven, ask the Savior: "Lord wilt thou at this time restore the kingdom . . . ?" Yes, that is what Jesus does in fact today, though admittedly in a sense not meant by the questioners. For today the Lord, and with Him His human nature, has entered into the glory of the Father and shares in His kingship over heaven and earth and the regions below. Today the Father says to Him: "Sit thou at my right hand, until [on the last day] I make thy enemies thy footstool!" (Ps. 109:1.) On earth "he humbled himself [the Son of God], becoming obedient unto death. For which cause God also hath [today] exalted him and hath given him a name which is above all names" (Phil. 2:7 ff.). All that is in heaven and on earth and under the earth must bow the knee before Him and be subject to Him, angel and man and devil alike. All must order their lives according to His will. The concluding part of the *Lesson* confirms the promise of the angels: In the end Christ will come again, to judge the living and the dead.

In the *Alleluia* the jubilation breaks out afresh: "The Lord [is ascended] with the sound of trumpet." What were they, these trumpets that sounded as Jesus ascended into heaven? The Fathers take them to mean the voices of the angels that greeted the King of Glory at the threshold of heaven. "Vox tubae — vox angelorum," says Augustine (cf. Ps. 46:6). "The Lord is ascended on high, he hath led captivity captive, Alleluia." Up to that time heaven, the abode of ineffable bliss, had remained closed. Today Christ enters, the first to do so, bringing with Him the souls of the holy men and women of the Old Testament. Also of the number is, for example, St. Joseph. The angels gaze in wonder at Christ, the vanquisher of death and hell, returning in triumph with a portion of the spoils that He has wrested from Satan by His redemptive death. He has delivered mankind, enslaved by sin, from its chains.

In the *Gospel* Mark briefly reports the *fact* of the ascension of Jesus: "after he had spoken to them" [given them once more the command to go and preach the gospel], he was taken up into heaven, and sitteth on the right hand of God." (To symbolize the homecoming of Jesus into heaven, the Easter candle, which represents the Resurrection, is today extinguished after the *Gospel*.) The Evangelists Matthew and Luke have also left us their account of the ascension of Jesus. That of Luke closes with the moving words: "And they [the Apostles] adoring went back into Jerusalem with great joy." They rejoiced primarily for Jesus, for now, after His life of hardship and self-denial, and after His terrible passion, He is to enter into eternal glory and take possession of His throne, from which to rule the world. How we too rejoice over it from our hearts and manifest to the Savior our special joy that we should be intimately sharing in the jubilation of today's festival Mass! But we rejoice also for ourselves at the exaltation of Christ. As Leo I expressed it in a sermon: "Our human nature [in the manhood of Jesus] was raised above all the hosts of heaven, exalted even beyond the choirs of angels. It was permitted to ascend unconstrained to the very throne of God, there to alight and share in the glory of Him with whose nature it had been united in the

Son of God. . . . Let us therefore rejoice, for on this day heaven has become our possession." It is in this sense that the Church prays in the *Communicantes* before the *Consecration:* "In the unity of holy fellowship, celebrating the most sacred day on which your only-begotten Son our Lord, placed at the right hand of your glory the substance of our frail human nature which he had taken to himself." Though free Himself from concupiscence, the Son of God knows from experience the weakness of our human nature; before the Father He makes our cause His cause, and our care His care. Unceasingly He offers Himself to the Father for us, and prepares a place for us, that where He is we may also be (Jn. 13:3 ff.).

Today too, He who sits at the right hand of the Father prays for us at the *Consecration,* that we may receive all the graces we stand in need of, so that later we may be with Him. Both in the *Epistle* and in the *Gospel* we are told today that before His Ascension Christ appeared to His disciples "as they were at table." In like manner He comes to us today at the table of the Eucharist, and, with the sacred bread which is His Body, plants in us the seed of immortality and glorious resurrection. Grant that when we come to the end of our days He may also appear to us "at table" as the Holy Viaticum and lead us home to the Father. "Sing to the Lord, who ascendeth above the heaven of heavens to the east, alleluia!" (*Communion hymn*).

SUNDAY AFTER THE FEAST
OF THE ASCENSION

Yearning After Christ and the Spirit of the Comforte

IN ITS whole character today's feast is a transition from the feast of the Ascension of Christ to the feast of Pentecost which we are to celebrate next week. It is an echo of the Ascension and a preparation for Pentecost, and the liturgy of this day is marked by great fervor and depth of feeling. What a difference between today's texts and those of the Ascension! On the feast of the Ascension of Jesus into heaven we rejoiced at the glory and the happiness that were His — today we feel ourselves abandoned by Him, and, at the very beginning of the Mass (*Introit*) we pray with longing lamentation: "Hear, O Lord, my voice. . . . Thy face, O Lord, will I still seek!" With the Apostles we gaze unceasingly up to heaven, seeking the face of Jesus. Christ, have mercy on us! Whoever lives a truly interior life will experience periods when he seeks the face of God but does not find it. He feels a constant yearning for God, and for a life in His presence; but God, who previously had inundated his soul with comfort when he prayed seems as it were to hide Himself and will not let Himself be found. The soul feels spiritually empty and arid, and derives no comfort from prayer; in creatures, too, it finds no consolation and does not even seek it there. It is indifferent to all earthly things. This is a testing by God, and the beginning of great subsequent graces. The only thing to do is courageously to persevere, and to remain faithful to God even in the midst of dryness and dark night and abandonment, even when perhaps at the same time great storms arise in the soul or God visits one with sickness. We must watch without ceasing for the face of God and pray: Lord, have mercy on us; Christ, have mercy on us! "Hear, O Lord, my voice . . . thy face, O Lord, will I still seek."

In the jubilant *Gloria,* too, the petition that today ascends most fervently from our hearts, homesick for Christ is: "Who sits at the right hand of the Father, have mercy upon us!" Without the Savior we feel ourselves isolated on this earth. "O Jesus, you are my delight, without you there is only sorrow." Let us but say to Him often as an earnest of our sincere love: "Your presence, O Lord, I still seek!" It would indeed be a fitting ejaculation for today and the next few days. Yes, our whole life, like that of the early Christians, must be filled with nostalgic love of Christ.

In this conviction we are resolved — in the words of the *Collect* — "ever to have a will devoted to thee, and to serve thy majesty with a sincere heart." Especially with love of our neighbor, in conformity with the words of Jesus: "As long as you did it to one of these my least brethren, you did it to me." To our plaintive "thy face, O Lord, I still seek," Jesus answers: You will find it in the face of your brothers and sisters. Since Jesus is no longer visibly among us we must show Him our love in the person of our neighbor. To this we are exhorted by the Apostle Peter in today's *Epistle:* "Dearly beloved, . . . have a constant mutual charity among yourselves!" In the countenance of our neighbor we must seek Christ. And this is also the best preparation for Pentecost, for the Holy Spirit is in fact the spirit of love.

And behold, after the *Lesson,* as if to reward our good resolutions, the voice of Jesus comes down to us from heaven, where He "reigns on his throne, as God, over all the nations." He turns His face to us from heaven and says: "I will not leave you orphans; I will come to you" — namely in the person of the Holy Spirit whom He sends us in His stead as Comforter (*Easter Alleluia*). In the *Gospel* He promises us expressly: "When the Paraclete cometh, whom I will send you from the Father, . . . he shall give testimony of me, and you also shall give testimony." And immediately Jesus explains more fully in what this testimony consists: in true fidelity to Him even to the point of heroic readiness in times of persecution to give one's blood for Christ. "The hour cometh, when whosoever killeth you, will think that he doth a service to God. . . . These things I have told you, that, when the hour shall come, you may remember that I told you of them." The Apostles were able, and we also are able, to give testimony of Christ in this way only by virtue of the grace of the Holy Spirit whom Jesus sends down to that end. Hence we yearn for the Holy Spirit and during these weeks pray with special fervor for His coming.

In truth, there is nothing sentimental about the love of Jesus for His own. It is a really virile love and it demands on their part the highest self-abnegation. To take upon oneself sacrifice and suffering for love of Jesus and for the salvation of souls is the highest perfection of love. He Himself has loved us with this heroic love which culminated in His death on the cross. And now His sacrificial death is about to be renewed here on the altar. In the celebration of Mass He makes us sharers of His will to sacrifice. By His union with us in Holy Communion He makes us strong against our enemies and for the conquering of evil (*Communion hymn*). In deep earnest let us ask of the Savior today: Send us, O Lord, the Spirit of the Comforter, that He may bring us strength and that our life, whatever may befall, may never be anything but a testimony for Thee, O Jesus.

WHITSUNDAY

"And They Were All Filled With the Holy Ghost!"

ONE day during World War II the doctor entered a hospital ward and asked sarcastically: What is it that you Catholics mean when you celebrate Pentecost today? There was no answer.

It is something essentially new that happened at Jerusalem at Pentecost and that continues to happen ever since without interruption. In the time before Christ the grace of the Holy Spirit operated to only a very small extent. But since the first Feast of Pentecost it has flowed out in rich measure over all the faithful for the building up of the Church established by Christ. Thus are fulfilled the words of the Prophet Joel (2:28 ff.) to which Peter refers in the Epistle of Ember Wednesday in Whitsun week: "And it shall come to pass in the last days, saith the Lord, that I will pour out my Spirit upon all flesh: and your sons and your daughters shall prophesy and your young men shall see visions. . . . And I will show wonders."

What we have commemorated so far in the ecclesiastical year, from Advent to the Ascension of Christ into heaven, has been the life of Jesus and the work of redemption through which He earned and stored up grace for us. But the Church of Jesus did not yet exist and the Apostles lived in hiding. So today Christ completes His work by sending down from heaven the Holy Spirit who is the soul of the Church. Now it became a living Church. The Apostles preached, and on this day alone baptized three thousand people. At Pentecost the grace merited by Christ accrues to all the faithful; the grace of the Holy Spirit is poured out upon all flesh (cf. Acts 10:45). Now the newly founded Church stands at the side of her bridegroom, Christ, who celebrates His marriage with her in the Holy Spirit by letting His spirit stream into His Church, thus breathing divine life into mankind over the whole earth. "Send forth your spirit, and they shall be created [natural creatures shall receive divine life], and you shall renew the face of the earth." Pentecost is a supernatural re-creation of man. Now the Holy Spirit, who is the spirit of Christ, comes to take the place of Jesus and works in the whole of mankind until the end of time.

Pentecost, the fiftieth day after Easter, is not so much a separate feast as a completion and conclusion of the feast of Easter. It is the octave of Easter celebrated over a whole week. Then with the Saturday after Pentecost the Easter season proper ends. What was begun at Easter in baptism is completed at Pentecost in confirmation with the descent of the Holy Spirit. The baptized Christian must now by the power of the Holy Spirit give testimony for Christ like the Apostles. Easter is the renewal of baptism, Pentecost the renewal of confirmation.

The Station-church today is St. Peter's. We gather round the first Pope for the celebration of the most holy feast of Pentecost. With him and the other Apostles, in the room of the Last Supper, we longingly await the coming of the Holy Spirit.

❉   ❉   ❉

The text of the *Introit* is drawn from the working of the Holy Spirit in nature. At the creation of the world, we are told in the Scripture, the spirit of God moved over the waters. He is the creative genius, the life-giver, who fills the whole world with life. All our sighs and all our cares are known to Him. "The spirit of the Lord hath filled the whole world; and that, which containeth all things, hath knowledge of the voice." Therefore let us give glory to the Father, the Son, and the Holy Spirit! Because He is also present in us He hears our earnest supplication: Lord, have mercy on us! Christ, have mercy on us! Lord, have mercy on us!

The *Collect* is a transition from the natural to the supernatural working of the Holy Spirit. Just as in nature the sun diffuses light and warmth, so we pray that the Holy Spirit may supernaturally enlighten our understanding and fill our hearts with comforting love. "Grant that by the light of the Holy Spirit we may relish what is right, and ever rejoice in his consolation." May He awaken in us divine life!

In the *Lesson*, which is taken from the Acts of the Apostles, we are given a vivid description of the historic miracle of Pentecost. The members of the infant Church, orphaned since the Ascension, are assembled in the room of the Last Supper, with Mary in their midst. Fervently, they pray to the Holy Spirit, the "other Comforter." Then, about the third hour (9 a.m.), a mighty wind sweeps through the house like a hurricane. Fiery tongues appear above the head of each one of them, and they are all filled with the Holy Spirit. This manifests itself even outwardly when, in a transport of holy zeal, they all begin to speak in strange tongues. May the holy fire of Pentecost come to our soul also at this hour, even though it be invisibly! In celebrating Pentecost the liturgy has in mind not just something out of the past, but, primarily, something that is taking place here and now.

Therefore, at the *Alleluia*, which we say upon our knees, we pray that the miracle of Pentecost may be repeated in us today. "Come, O Holy Spirit, fill the hearts of your faithful, and kindle in them the fire of your love." In the magnificent *Sequence*, which is a prolongation of the "Veni Sancte Spiritus" of the Alleluia verse, we invoke the Holy Spirit under a great variety of imagery: Be thou light for the darkness of our soul, comforter in suffering, soothing coolness in the heat of passion, freshening dew in the hours of spiritual dryness. To thy sweet yoke our stiff necks bow. Warm with thy love our hearts of snow. Our wandering feet recall. Finally, we pray for the seven gifts of the Holy Spirit.

In the *Gospel* Jesus Himself describes the working of the Holy Spirit in our soul. Together with the Father and the Son He comes and takes up His abode in our hearts, makes of us His temple. "We will come . . . and make our abode. . . ." Thus present in our innermost being the Holy Spirit will speak to us and enlighten our spirit: "He will teach you all things." As Comforter He brings great interior joy to our soul: "Peace I leave with you, my peace I give to you," a peace and a happiness that the world cannot conceive. Let us truly yearn for such a spirit and pray today without ceasing: "Come, Holy Spirit!"

In the *Offertory* we are reminded that at Easter by baptism, we have joined the generation of the "elect," the race of "kings." And so we now approach the altar and pray for the completion of the grace of baptism, for the consolidation of the work of Easter. "Confirm, O God, what thou hast wrought in us; . . . kings [we ourselves] shall offer presents to thee."

Finally, in the *Communion*, the miracle of Pentecost is re-enacted in our soul. For Jesus brings the Holy Spirit, who proceeds from Him and comes to us in the shape of fire and wind, though silently hidden in the white Host. That is what the Church intends to convey in the antiphon that is recited at the distribution of Communion: "There came a sound from heaven . . . and they were all filled with the Holy Ghost."

TRINITY SUNDAY

Praise and Thanks Be to the Triune God!

LET us pause for a moment on our journey through the ecclesiastical year to see precisely where we stand. With the Saturday within the Octave of Pentecost we closed the season of Easter proper. One outward sign of this will be that from now on the number of Alleluias will be once more reduced. Today we enter on the so-called post-Pentecostal season which lasts for half a year. But this season is not, as was formerly thought, a distinct third cycle of feasts — the Pentecost Cycle of Feasts they called it — which was supposed to follow on the Christmas and Easter cycles as an independent part of the ecclesiastical year. More correctly, if we must use this designation by cycles, the period that begins today belongs to the Easter Cycle. In fact the feast of Pentecost itself together with its octave is nothing else than a sort of grand octave day of the feast of Easter.

The purport of the post-Pentecostal liturgy is preservation of what we have received at baptism (Easter) and confirmation (Pentecost). In this period the Christian must prove himself in his ordinary everyday earthly life and constantly press on to the goal of fulfillment until the harvest day of the second coming of Christ at the last judgment (last Sunday after Pentecost). It is the silent time of the whole year; it embraces twenty-four weeks, and more, since the balance of the Sundays after the Epiphany are also incorporated. In this period the divine life that was established in us at Easter must be reinforced and extended. Christ has gone before us into heaven to prepare a place for us. And then "I will come again, and will take you to myself; that where I am, you also may be" (Jn. 14:3).

Thus today we celebrate in itself the First Sunday after Pentecost. But, ever since the fourteenth century, the liturgy of the First
Sunday after Pentecost has been supplanted by the Feast of the
Most Holy Trinity. The Sunday itself can be carried over to the first
free day of this week. — And what is the meaning and purpose of
the Feast of the Trinity? Briefly it is nothing else than to offer our
homage to the Triune God and to give Him thanks for all the
blessings that He has sent us.

All that we possess in the way of natural and supernatural goods
has been given to us by the Holy Trinity. The Father created us
out of nothing, together with the whole universe around and above
us; the Son became man and redeemed us; and the Holy Spirit
interiorly sanctified us. These great blessings of God, each in its
turn, have been commemorated already in the liturgy of the
ecclesiastical year: the Father, who created us and the world, wished
to raise us up again to supernatural life after we had fallen from
grace through the sin of Adam. Therefore He "has not spared even
his own Son," but sent Him into the world, Him for whom the
whole world had been yearning for thousands of years. Of all this
we are reminded at the beginning of the ecclesiastical year, in the
season of Advent. At Christmas the Son of God was born to us;
He grew up among men, and redeemed us by His death and resurrection. Then, at Pentecost, He sent down from the Father the
Holy Spirit with His wonderful gifts of grace, to be, after Jesus
had gone from us, our guide to heaven. For all these immeasurable
blessings we give thanks today and offer praise to the Triune God
in His majesty and greatness as particularly manifested in the profound mystery of the Trinity. Today's feast is, as it were, a *Te
Deum* after all the great feasts of the Church, a synopsis of Christmas, Easter, and Pentecost.

✻   ✻   ✻

Every Sacrifice of the Mass begins at the steps of the altar with
a dedication to the Trinity: "In the name of the Father, and of the
Son, and of the Holy Spirit." Let us today say the words with
special devoutness and make the accompanying sign of the cross
with more than usual reverence. In the *Introit* the aim — already
explained — of today's feast and today's Mass is further stressed:
"Blessed be the holy Trinity and undivided Unity: we will give

glory to him, because he hath shown his mercy to us." And the concluding verse of the psalm reminds us particularly how wonderfully the Father in heaven, for love of us, created also the world of nature: "O Lord, our Lord, how admirable is thy name." With deepest reverence we pray: "Glory be to the Father. . . ."

At the *Kyrie* today we ask the Father, Son, and Holy Spirit to pardon us if we have hitherto shown ourselves too little thankful for their countless blessings or have even repaid them with sin and error. — The *Gloria* is itself the most beautiful hymn of praise and thanks to the Triune God; it is — as also the *Credo* — built up on the Trinity, that is to say, it is addressed in turn to the Father, Son, and Holy Spirit. — The *Collect* refers to the two central themes of our mystery: the glorious, harmonious Trinity, and the powerful Unity.

In the *Epistle*, filled with wonder and adoring awe, we stand with Paul before the most unfathomable mystery of our Faith, incomprehensible to our human intelligence: three Persons, and yet but one single divine nature; Father, Son, and Holy Spirit, each truly God, and yet only one God. The Son proceeds from the mind of the Father, being generated in the Father's self-knowledge; the Holy Spirit proceeds from the mutual love of Father and Son. "O the depths of the riches of the wisdom and of the knowledge of God! How incomprehensible are his judgments, and how unsearchable his ways! . . . Of him [the Father] and by him [the Son] and in him [the Holy Spirit] are all things. To him be glory for ever. Amen." The *Gradual* carries on the praises of the last phrase of the Lesson in a threefold direction: Blessed be God in the depths of the sea, blessed in the firmament of heaven where He reigns over the cherubim, blessed in the destiny of men which in our fathers and ancestors He guided from generation to generation.

In the *Gospel* Christ Himself, in limpid words, attests the mystery of the Most Holy Trinity: "Going therefore, teach ye all nations, baptizing them in the name of the Father, and of the Son, and of the Holy Spirit." In the earliest days of Christianity the recipients of baptism had to be completely immersed in water. The significance of it was this: in baptism our souls are immersed in the mystical lifestream of the Father, Son, and Holy Spirit, and so made partakers of the divine nature (cf. 2 Pet. 1:4). Through it we acquired a title to heaven, a title to be admitted to the enjoyment of the divine life hereafter. For this we give thanks once more in the *Offertory:* "Blessed be God the Father, and the only-begotten Son of God, and also the Holy Spirit, because he has shown his mercy to us." Herein lies the great beauty and the characteristic feature of today's Mass: for ourselves we ask nothing; the Triune God alone stands in the foreground, and to Him we offer our thanks and praise.

In the thrice-repeated *Sanctus,* in union with the angels and saints, we adore the Triune God. At the *Consecration* praise and thanks are rendered to Him, no longer merely through our feeble words, for now the Son of God appears on the altar and, in our name, as man, offers to the Father and the Holy Spirit the great Sacrifice of praise and thanks and expiation. Then in the Communion we carry Christ in our breast and, in union with Him, we make the Mass ring out in the *Communion hymn* with praise and thanks just as we did at the beginning: "We will praise the God of heaven . . . because he hath shown his mercy to us."

CORPUS CHRISTI

"Do This in Memory of Me"

THE name of this feast means the Body of Christ, that is, the Body of our Lord Jesus Christ as present in the Eucharist.

What is the meaning of the feast? Let us imagine for a moment that the Savior had instituted all the other sacraments, but not the Sacrament of the Altar. There would then be no Mass, no Communion, and during the day Jesus would not be present in our churches. How desolate and miserable we would feel! The heart would have gone out of Christianity. But in fact, thanks to the Savior, He is really and uninterruptedly with us, offers Himself up for us daily in the Mass, and even comes into our breast at Holy Communion. To render Him our heartfelt praise and thanks for these gifts we celebrate Corpus Christi with great gladness and rejoicing. Hence the many Alleluias in the Mass, the same as at Easter time through the feast falls outside that season. It is true that the Mass texts of Maundy Thursday too draw their inspiration from the Most Holy Sacrament which was instituted at the Last Supper, but there the passion of Jesus is too present in our minds to permit of joyful exultation. That is why Pope Urban IV, in the year 1246, prescribed the present feast for the whole Church.

*   *   *

Because of this singleness of object of the feast — the Body of Jesus in the Eucharist — the Mass texts of themselves reveal a harmonious unity. In the separate parts the various attributes and workings of this sacrament are set forth, unfolding the mystery for us in all its fullness.

In the Old Testament God nourished His chosen people, in their wandering through the desert, with manna, a miraculous "bread from heaven!" And from a rock — which according to Paul (1 Cor. 10:4), was a symbol of Christ — in marvelous manner He provided them with water. Even more marvelously does Christ provide for His people of the New Testament, for us Christians in our pilgrimage toward heaven: He has given Himself to be our food, a sustaining and at the same time a sweet and blessed food: "He fed them with the finest wheat, and filled them with honey from the rock, Alleluia!" (*Introit*). (In the East the honey sometimes flows from rocks in the crevices of which the bees have nested.) In Holy Communion Jesus gives us strength to live uprightly ("wheat") and sweet comfort in our earthly sorrows ("honey"). Therefore let us "sing aloud to God, our Savior!"

The *Collect* is full of moving thoughts. It calls the Eucharist a "wonderful sacrament," since for its realization a whole series of wonders is necessary. Bread and wine are changed into the Body and Blood of Christ. The incarnate God is present in the little particle of bread, spiritualized somehow, and yet preserving His true human nature. He is consumed by us without thereby being impaired. Even if the Hosts are divided He is still fully present in each part. Truly, "what can be more wonderful than this sacrament?" Through the separation of body and blood it represents the passion of Jesus. "O God [we say to Jesus], in this wonderful Sacrament you have left us a memorial of your passion." For in the Host, symbolically regarded, is contained only His dead body, and in the chalice His blood that was shed on the cross. "Do this in memory" of My passion! The Eucharist embraces the bloody sacrifice of the cross with all the sufferings and indignities that accompanied it: the sweat of blood on the Mount of Olives, the scourging at the pillar, the crowning with thorns, the sublime renunciation, the obedience and the unquestioning surrender to the will of the Father, His immeasurable love for us sinners — all of this we humbly and adoringly revere in the Holy Eucharist. It is a sacred funeral feast at which we are given the Flesh and Blood of Jesus to eat. With what devotion we should do this! But we mortals succumb so easily to routine and place so little value on what we can every day enjoy! Hence we address to the Savior Himself in the sacrament the request: "Grant us so to venerate the sacred mysteries that we may evermore feel within us the fruit of thy redemption."

In the *Epistle* Paul tells us factually how Jesus instituted this most holy sacrament at the Last Supper for all time. He handed the Apostles bread and wine with the words: "This is my body . . . my blood." Then He went on: "Do this in memory of me." Thereby He transmitted to the Apostles and their successors the power to do as He had done, namely to change bread into His body and wine into His blood, to celebrate Mass and to give Holy Communion. By the one sentence were the priesthood and the Eucharist instituted.

The *Gradual* gives us first a text from the Old Testament, followed by one from the New. The first speaks of the natural food that God provides with open hand for all His hungry creatures. In the New Testament Jesus Himself is the supernatural food of our soul: "My flesh is food, indeed, and my blood is drink indeed!"

In the *Sequence,* with which this great feast is specially marked, the Church, through the mouth of her greatest theologian, St. Thomas Aquinas, imparts to us a most detailed dogmatic instruction on the mystery of the Eucharist.

In the *Gospel* Christ appears before us and tells us of the fruits of Holy Communion. "He who eats [me] abides in me and I in him." There results a mysterious union between our soul and the divinity of Jesus. St. Cyril of Jerusalem makes the comparison: "Pour molten wax into molten wax and they will mix completely. In like manner does Christ merge in us and we in Him." As I live because of the Father, so "He who eats me, he also shall live because of me." In the Communion there takes place an inexpressible fusion of ourselves with Christ. Christ unites His divine life and the life of our soul into one single common life, just as between the heavenly Father and His Son there is but one life. What a sublime and unfathomable mystery it is that we have in Holy Communion!

Without a priest there can be no sacrifice, and in the Holy Sacrifice of the Mass Christ Himself is the priest. But all the faithful must unite with Christ, the Priest-Victim, to offer the Lamb of sacrifice to the Father in heaven. Through baptism all the faithful are called to this service and are become "royal priests." Therefore they must be free from sin. Of all this we are reminded by the *Offertory hymn* ("The priests of the Lord . . .").

What we have just been pondering now becomes full reality on the altar in the *Consecration* and the *Communion*. In order to assist at the Holy Sacrifice of the Mass and receive Communion worthily, so far as this is at all possible for a sinful mortal, we must, from the very beginning of the Mass, repent of our sins with all our hearts, bearing in mind the warning of the *Communion hymn:* "Whosoever eats this bread . . . unworthily, will be guilty of the body . . . of the Lord."

SECOND SUNDAY AFTER PENTECOST

"Come Ye All to the Great Supper!"

As ALREADY pointed out last Sunday the whole aim of all the twenty-four Sundays after Pentecost is to develop the paschal, that is to say the divine, life in our soul. In the midst of the battle of life we must preserve and augment the divine life we received in baptism and confirmation. Thus we advance with Christ in the love of the Holy Spirit to meet the Father, until the day when Christ comes again and leads us home to the eternal dwelling of the Father.

The Sundays after Pentecost have therefore three essential motifs that keep recurring, each in its turn being stressed above the others: the first is the looking back to Easter. Every Sunday is a kind of

Easter in that we cause to be revived within us the happiness of Easter with its baptism, confirmation, and Eucharist. We renew our renunciation of Satan and our dedication to Christ. Thus we seek to repair our strength for the struggle of our present life, that we may preserve ourselves always as true Christians. The third motif looks ahead into the future, to the coming of Christ for the judgment.

The first six Sundays look back more to Easter and aim at bringing our life of grace to an ever greater expansion. The miraculous healings of Jesus, of which we are told on these Sundays, are meant to represent the grace-giving power of the Mass of the Sunday in question. Just as Christ once healed bodies, so now, through the mystery of the Mass and the Eucharist, does He heal our souls. In the Mass texts of the Seventh to the Fourteenth Sundays the struggle motif predominates, the kingdom of God being continually contrasted with the kingdom of the world. Even for the baptized two paths remain always open: the path of life and the path of death. Toward the end of the ecclesiastical year, from the Fifteenth Sunday (Autumn Ember Days) onward, we prepare ourselves for the coming of the Judge of the world; the thought of the last judgment is then uppermost.

The Church (that is, we) "has now truly entered with the transfigured Lord into the timeless world of God and leads with Him a celestial existence. Hence the Sundays after Pentecost are stamped with the manifold wondrous calm of the transfiguration; they breathe the air of eternity. But the Church lives the new heavenly life while still set in its earthly receptacle of corporeality and temporality. It is still assailable by the world of the devil. Hence the liturgy of the post-Pentecostal season frequently resounds with cries of battle, calls for rescue and impassioned supplication. Thus the second half of the ecclesiastical year bears the twofold character of stirring combat and transfigured calm, but yet in such a manner that the stamp of calm is always the predominating one" (A. Loehr).

*   *   *

Today's Mass affords a good example of how the three motifs we have mentioned are closely interwoven. The *Introit* reminds us of our redemption at Easter: "The Lord became my protector. And he brought me forth into a large place: he saved me, because

he was well pleased with me. I will love thee, O Lord, my strength!"
In loving homage we then say: "Glory be to the Father. . . ." That
is the right approach to God: on the one hand childlike love, and
on the other just as childlike awe. So much does God love us, and
we Him, that He remains always for us not only our Father but
our Lord as well. Therefore in the *Collect* we pray for both of these
dispositions: "Make us, O Lord, to have a perpetual fear and love
of thee." That is, in the first place, a firm and solid love that will
not easily waver. When we have it we can be certain that God will
ever lovingly guide our destiny.

While the question so far has been our love of God, the beginning of the *Epistle* now speaks of the hatred that is in the world.
The creatures of the world hate one another, and hate, in particular,
the followers of Jesus. Here the motif of Easter gives place to the
struggle motif. We Christians must conquer ourselves; we must love
even our enemies, but still more our fellow Christians. Truly magnificent, but not easy to put into execution, are the words that that
great teacher of charity, the Apostle John, addresses to us: "Whosoever hateth his brother is a murderer. . . . In this we have known
the charity of God, because he hath laid down his life for us: and
we ought to lay down our lives for the brethren. . . . My little
children, let us not love in word, nor in tongue, but in deed, and
in truth." All through our lives it is going to cost us an effort to be
faithful to the commandment to love our neighbor, which is next
in importance to the commandment to love God. Let us examine
ourselves today and see how we stand in regard to it.

Then, at the *Gradual,* conscious of our weakness, we fervently
pray for God's help in the fulfillment of this commandment: "In
my trouble I cry to the Lord. . . . Deliver me from wicked lips [not
forgetting to give thought to our own]. . . . Save me!"

The *Gospel* treats of the great love of God for us. He invites all
mankind to the great supper. Since we are near the feast of Corpus
Christi we may be inclined to take this to mean immediately and
exclusively the Eucharist. But in fact this parable of Jesus in the
Second Sunday after Pentecost was being read hundreds of years
before there was any Feast of Corpus Christi. The supper to which
God invites all certainly includes the Eucharist (Mass, Communion,
Adoration of the Blessed Sacrament), but over and above this it is
also, and primarily, the kingdom of God in general: the prospect of

eternal salvation, the incarnation, the redemption, baptism and all the other sacraments, the various graces and means of grace, the Church, and, finally, the great wedding feast in heaven. But a great part of mankind have no desire to hear about this infinite divine love which has prepared for us this wonderful banquet. They think up all possible kinds of excuses for staying away from the festive table. It is for them that the terrible threat of the last sentence to today's Gospel is intended: "I say unto you that none of those men . . . shall taste of my supper!" That is to say, none of them will be admitted to take a place at the blessed wedding feast in heaven. The Judge will say to them: "Depart from me into the fire, I know you not." Here we have a recurrence of the motif of the coming again of Jesus for the judgment.

In the *Offertory hymn* we implore that we may not be of the number of these men: "Turn to me, O Lord. . . . Save me!"

Today, now at Mass, Christ comes at the *Consecration* as the great Provider and prepares, for us particularly, the eucharistic banquet of the *Communion*. Eagerly we accept His invitation. Of our very nature we are unworthy of this mystical feast. As poor sinners we belong to the beggars and the cripples, the blind and the lame. But precisely for that reason Jesus, out of His great love, invites us to the feast. And when we then partake of it we rejoice thankfully in the *Communion hymn* at the end of the Mass: "I will sing to the Lord, who giveth me good things . . . and I will sing to the name of the Lord most high."

FEAST OF THE SACRED HEART OF JESUS

At the Fountainhead of Grace and Mercy!

WHAT do we celebrate today? What does the Church understand by "Sacred Heart of Jesus"? Our physical heart — the heart in the literal sense — is an entirely internal organ, invisible from without. From it we draw life; it is the motive power of all physical being, the central organ that is always at work and that participates in all the actions of men. Similarly, in the life of the spirit all external acts proceed from the interior and the invisible: from our silent thoughts, principles, sentiments, impulses of fear, hope, love, aversion. That is the "heart" in the figurative sense. Thus we speak of a heart that is noble, pure, faithful, motherly, and so on. Accordingly, by the "Sacred Heart of Jesus" we mean the entire, incarnate, holy, spiritual life of our Lord and all the virtues. His whole interior life, therefore; His holy wishes and impulses, His humility, purity, dedication to the Father, His piety, zeal, inexhaustible love of men, His poverty, patience, meekness, His valor and steadfastness in difficult hours.

Out of this infinitely rich interior life flowed His words and deeds, above all out of His charity, which is the queen of all the virtues. Out of this profoundest love He came down from heaven, became man: led a life of poverty and obedience, labored untiringly among men for three long years to save them for heaven, died on the cross, ascended into heaven to send us down the Holy Spirit, and remains with us in the Sacrament of the Altar. These outpourings of the Sacred Heart we celebrate today with a special feast. They are indeed the fount of all the great works of Jesus that we have met with in the feasts of the ecclesiastical year up to the present. Our feast day today is a feast of inwardness, an exhortation to a holy interior life, out of which holy deeds will grow of themselves.

*   ⚬   ✿

The *Introit* reveals the inmost workings of the heart of our Redeemer: His whole thought and mind are centered unbrokenly on saving all men for eternal happiness. "But the counsel of the Lord standeth for ever: the thoughts of his heart to all generations. To deliver their souls from death, and feed them in famine." This last promise Jesus fulfills mainly through the Sacrament of the Altar. The feast of the Sacred Heart of Jesus follows shortly after the feast of Corpus Christi. How fitting this is.

Now the *Collect* presents to us a vivid picture of the Heart of Jesus: the Savior is hanging on the cross and His heart is cleft wide open; it is our sins that have inflicted the wound; the water and blood that flow from it symbolize the inestimable treasures of grace that the Sacred Heart has procured for us by His death on the cross. And the thank offering that is demanded of us in return is loving devotion and atonement. Loving devotion means the dedication of our whole being and of all our powers and faculties to Jesus. We resign everything to Him and ask that He may do with us according to His will. Jesus Himself has said: "He who has my commandments and keeps them, he it is who loves me" (Jn. 14:21). Therefore "let us control our senses; let us moderate even our innocent satisfactions. Let us detach ourselves inwardly, and even outwardly so far as our calling permits, from creature things. Let us unite our will in perfect conformity with His pleasure. . . . O happy we if He should wound our soul with His love so that it loses all relish for everything that is not Him" (Baur). And where there is true love there is naturally also atonement. Our own sins and those of our fellow creatures afflict us with pain because they are directed against Jesus and cause Him suffering. We ask His pardon. We are honestly grieved that so many do not know Him or wish to know Him. All the more, therefore, do we strive after perfect fidelity and, in that spirit, take upon ourselves sacrifice and suffering. "*O amore non conosciuto!* O love unknown!" — as St. Mary Magdalen of Pazzi kept sighing, her gaze fixed on the cross. True veneration of the Sacred Heart has nothing of fulsomeness about it. It is a training for valiant carrying of the cross.

From the *Epistle* of St. Paul streams forth ardent love of the Sacred Heart. This man of action is not ashamed openly to avow his tender love of Jesus. He declares that to him was given the mission to preach to the entire world "the unfathomable riches of Christ," which have their source in the Heart of Jesus: membership of His mystical body and, through it, participation in His divine life even here on earth with the assurance of participation in His happiness in eternity. That is, as the Apostle concludes by saying, the ever incomprehensible "breadth and length and height and depth, and to know Christ's love which surpasses all knowledge." Hence the exhortation: "in order that you may be filled into all the fullness of God."

Stirred by these profoundly moving words of the Apostle we lift up our gaze to the Sacred Heart and sing to Him in the *Gradual* a song of praise: "The Lord is kind and sweet . . . he teaches the meek his way." In answer we receive from the sweet Heart of Jesus the invitation: "Learn from me, for I am meek and humble of heart; and you will find rest for your souls." — Whereas in all the other texts of the Mass there is mention only of charity, here we find extolled also the other virtues of the Most Sacred Heart: righteousness, meekness, humility. The Sacred Heart is "the fount of all the virtues."

The *Gospel* takes us back to the first beginning of the honoring of the Sacred Heart of Jesus. The Apostle John relates as an eyewitness how, on the cross, the heart of Jesus — even the corporeal heart of the Savior is the object of our veneration — was pierced. The blood and water that flow from it are a symbol of the Eucharist, and of baptism, and of all the graces that since then have streamed without intermission over the earth to the salvation of men for heaven.

In the *Offertory* Jesus Himself summons us to repentance, which has already been enjoined on us by the *Collect:* in the midst of the insults and suffering that are caused to His Heart by ungrateful men He looks for souls "to sympathize with me, but there was none." Let us assure the Savior that us at least He will find ready. By faithful love and sacrifice, O Savior, we shall comfort Thee, as did the angel in the Garden of Olives.

The Heart of Jesus was opened on the cross, that from it streams of mercy and grace might flow out over us. Now at Mass these streams begin to flow for us afresh. In the *Consecration* and the *Communion* we draw from them grace after grace. Of this we are reminded in the *Communion hymn:* "One of the soldiers opened his side with a lance, and immediately there came out blood and water." Let us then fervently pray to the Savior: "Hide me within thy wound [of the heart]; let me never be separated from thee!" There let us seek forever "the sacred treasury of divine bounty . . . a haven of peace" (*Preface*).

THIRD SUNDAY AFTER PENTECOST

Rejoice . . . Because I Have Found My Sheep That Was Lost!

THAT is the central theme of this Sunday. On the Second Sunday after Easter, too, we commemorated Christ the Good Shepherd who lays down His life for His sheep. Today He stands before us with the lost lamb on His shoulders. This is particularly well adapted to the Sunday which closely follows the Feast of the Sacred Heart: Christ, full of goodness and love for us poor sinners. For the first Christians this was, so to speak, their picture-of-the-Sacred-Heart. It is found over and over again in various catacombs: the Good Shepherd carries on his shoulders a lamb that was lost and that He has now found again; lovingly it twines itself round the neck of the Savior. The picture applies not only to the Christian who after baptism has fallen into mortal sin, but to all men; for, in Adam, all mankind were led astray and were left powerless to find their way to heaven unaided; they were like a lamb that could not find its way back to God's fold. But then the Son of God was moved to pity and came down to this vale of tears to snatch the lamb from the power of the wolf, that is to say, the devil. For thirty-three years in the midst of toil and privation He sought the lost one, and in the end it cost Him His life. "The good shepherd lays down his life for his sheep." In baptism man becomes once more a lamb that has been restored to the Good Shepherd who now leads it to rich pastures, and even nourishes it with His own flesh and blood. Thus Peter says to all Christians: "You were as sheep going astray, but you are now converted to the shepherd of your souls" (1 Pet. 2:25). All this applies in a very special way to a Christian who, after baptism, has fallen into mortal sin but returns to the Savior in the sacrament of penance.

o   o   o

Now at the Holy Mass, in deepest humility, we feel ourselves to be the lamb that has gone astray. In this conviction we raise our eyes, at the *Introit,* to the Good Shepherd and call out to Him: "Look thou upon me, and have mercy on me, O Lord, for I am alone and poor. See my abjection and my labor; and forgive me all my sins. To thee, O Lord, have I lifted up my soul. In thee, O my God, I put my trust." Lord, have mercy on us! In this same sense we have already prayed at the *Confiteor.*

In the *Gloria,* supplication of the Good Shepherd is again the central theme: "Who takes away the sins of the world, have mercy upon us . . . receive our prayer. Who sits at the right hand of the Father, have mercy upon us! Thou only art holy" — *we* cannot truly claim to be so.

These prayers have had reference to our past life. Looking to the future our greatest fear, even though we may now be in a state of grace, is lest we should once more be separated from the Good Shepherd through mortal sin. Hence the *Collect* of today reads: "O God, without whom is nothing strong and nothing holy, increase thy mercy upon us, that with thee for our ruler and our guide we may so pass through the good things of this life that we may not lose those of life everlasting."

In the *Epistle* we lambs of the fold of Christ are frightened by the roaring of the "lion, [who] goeth about seeking whom he may devour." The warning comes from Peter, the representative of the Good Shepherd. Indeed this Apostle had himself been for a time an erring sheep of Christ. But he had also himself experienced the unfathomable goodness of the Good Shepherd. So at the same time he comforts us and warns us against overanxiety: "casting all your care upon him, for he hath care of you." He will confirm you and establish you. If we heed the calls to grace of the Good Shepherd we shall be able to remain true to Him till death. In fact anyone who is deep-anchored in the faith and in charity knows no other anxiety than that he may at every moment do exactly what God would wish him to do. All else causes him no concern, for God is already taking care of it. These are the happiest souls, who leave everything that happens to them in life entirely to God.

And so the lost lamb, which a moment ago was trembling and bleating, is now filled with courage and trust, as we see in the *Gradual:* "I cried to the Lord; he hearkened to my voice from those that approach me. Alleluia! God is just and strong. . . ." To me too He will give strength and will not allow me to be tempted beyond my powers.

Then, in the *Gospel* — what a glorious climax! — we hear the voice of the Good Shepherd Himself. And truly it brings joyful tidings. A heart full of inexhaustible love for sinners speaks to us. In a parable He presents Himself to us as the Good Shepherd who goes in search of the sheep that was lost. When He finds it, He frees it with tender care from the thorns, takes it lovingly upon His shoulders and, though tired Himself from the long searching, carries it as a sweet burden back home. But that is not enough for His unimaginable love! He calls together His friends: "Rejoice with me, because I have found my sheep that was lost." And they all rejoice over it with the Good Shepherd: "There shall be joy in heaven over one sinner who repents, more than upon ninety-nine just who have no need of repentance." Were it not for the fact that these words are explicitly contained in the Bible, and that it was Christ Himself that spoke them, we should not dare to utter them. O unfathomable love of the Heart of Christ for us poor sinners! Let us then dare to utter them and to rejoice over them! The Savior Himself will have it so. And He was not content to let it go at beautiful words. He showed this love also in deeds; for instance toward the publicans, who in His day were looked upon as particularly great sinners; toward the woman taken in adultery, who had been turned away by the pharisees; toward the Samaritan woman; and especially toward the public prostitute. Let a man be weighed down under a mountain of sin, and still, if he repents, Christ lovingly presses him to His heart.

Filled with gratitude for this unheard of love, we sing in the *Offertory*: "Let them trust in thee . . . for thou hast not forsaken them that seek thee. Sing ye to the Lord. . . ." In our day too, Christ still goes looking for His poor lost sheep.

At the *Consecration* He appears among us to re-enact His giving of His life for us, His lambs. Nay more, He not only takes us upon His shoulders as His lost lamb, but unites Himself with us most interiorly. "He who eats my flesh, . . . abides in me and I in him." The angels of God, who cannot receive Communion, are struck with wonder at such boundless love and — as we read in the *Communion hymn* — there is joy before them "over one sinner who repents." Carrying with us this enchanting picture of the Good Shepherd we go out after the Mass — a truly beautiful Sacred-Heart-Mass — into the workaday world with happiness in our hearts.

FOURTH SUNDAY AFTER PENTECOST

Little Fishes of Christ!

THIS Sunday, mainly by reason of the gospel story of the great draught of fishes of the Apostle Peter, is closely connected with the feast day of that Saint, which is celebrated in these weeks. For the rest it is a proper Sunday after Pentecost with its three motifs of baptism, suffering and struggle, and yearning for the second coming of Christ.

The *Introit* brings our thoughts back to Easter, to our baptism. Every Sunday is a baptismal renewal. The very first words remind us of this: "The Lord is my light." The early Christians called baptism an "illumination through Christ." By baptism Christians become – as the Gospel of today puts it – little fishes of Christ. Tertullian (c. A.D. 200) says: "We are as little fishes, born in the water." We are taken up in the net of the Church, and thus come under the special protection of the Lord. "The Lord is my light and my salvation; whom shall I fear? The Lord is the protector of my life; of whom shall I be afraid? My enemies that trouble me have themselves been weakened and have fallen."

But as we are nevertheless conscious also of our weakness we ask, in the *Collect*, that God may shield the Church from its external enemies and give it tranquillity and peace: "Grant that the course of the world may be peaceably ordered for us by thy governance, and that thy church may rejoice in quiet devotion," that is to say, may apply itself unmolested to the liturgical worship of God.

And now, after the joyful Easter motif, the motif of suffering and struggle, already adumbrated in the Collect, breaks through in the *Epistle*. Paul speaks "of the sufferings of this time." Then he sets forth more particularly what sufferings he means. The whole material creation waits in longing expectation for "the revelation of the sons of God," that is to say, for the redemption. Even we "who have the first-fruits of the Spirit [namely baptism] . . . groan within ourselves." For despite baptism, and even if we are in a state of grace and therefore in fact redeemed, we remain constantly in

111

danger of falling into sin. We sigh and lament over the consequences of original sin: the many bodily pains that visit us all and the countless sufferings of the mind. Desire in a great variety of forms oppresses us. Sometimes it would seem as if all the good in us were dead. Joy in what is good seems to have deserted us. "The spirit is dull in prayer; the mind filled with hateful images; the memory as blank as if we had never received anything from God; the will inert and lifeless" (Baur). "One day our hearts are filled with zeal for God, the next we feel dragged down in a morass of sin. Today we feel ourselves free, tomorrow we slide back into our old slavery. . . . Now all is bright sunshine in us, and then once more black night. Today we rejoice with Peter: I shall never deny thee, Lord! On the morrow we have denied and betrayed Him thrice" (J. Engel). That is the way it is with man, made up as he is of the noble and the base, of spirit and of matter. Hence we must not falter in faith or in hope, nor weary of the struggle. Despite everything we Christians are filled with optimism. We "reckon that the sufferings of this time are not worthy to be compared with the glory to come, that shall be [after death, in heaven] revealed in us." It is by the will of God that we are subjected to these sufferings and miseries while we wait for the day of our final full redemption and transfiguration "through Jesus Christ our Lord." When He comes again on the last day — thus the second-coming motif is introduced at the end of the *Epistle* — then we shall be freed from all afflictions of body and soul and even the material world shall be transfigured. The last coming of the Lord is the beacon light in the darkness of the present.

Reflecting the more somber mood of the *Epistle* the *Gradual* rings out: "Forgive us our sins, O Lord . . . Help us." Nevertheless, in gladness and hope, we add to this supplication the Easter Alleluia.

That which the *Gospel* relates from the lifetime of Jesus becomes in a higher sense complete reality for all time, for today too, down to the last day. Christ went up into one of the ships, that belonged to Simon Peter. "And he taught the multitudes out of the ship." Today the ship is the Church, guided by the successor of Peter. Jesus Himself preaches to the multitudes; for the teaching that is preached by the infallible Church is still the pure teaching of Christ, proclaimed to all the world in His name. Then the Savior orders Simon and his companions to throw out the nets and gives them an abundant catch. "They enclosed a very great multitude of fishes." Jesus Himself said: That is a parable for the future. For "from henceforth thou shalt catch men." All the successors of the Apostles down to the present day are likewise fishers of men: popes, bishops, and priests. These very weeks are the season of ordinations and of the taking of first vows. It is Jesus Himself sending forth new fishers of men. Let us pray for them during Mass on these Sundays, that they may become worthy priests and that God may richly bless their draught of fishes.

At the *Consecration* the Master comes over to us from the shores of eternity. In the *Communion* He comes into our little ship, our fragile bark of life. We feel that we should say to Him with Peter: "Depart from me, for I am a sinful man, O Lord!" Lord, I am not worthy! But it is His will, that we receive Him. "Unless you eat the flesh of the Son of Man . . . you shall not have life in you." Filled with love, therefore, let us receive Him into our hearts, and then go forth into the world full of new confidence: "The Lord is my support, my refuge, and my deliverer; my God is my helper" (*Communion hymn*).

FIFTH SUNDAY AFTER PENTECOST

"Go First to Be Reconciled to Thy Brother, and Then Come and Offer Thy Gift"

It is remarkable how the texts of the Mass and their central themes differ from one Sunday to another, and what rich variety this gives to the liturgy. Two weeks ago, for instance, the Savior stood before us as the Good Shepherd, with the lamb on His shoulders. Last Sunday as the Fisherman gathering us Christians in a miraculous draught of fishes into the net of the Church. Today the liturgy of the Mass puts before us not a picture but a moral: Love one another! Love even your enemy who has done you wrong, and be reconciled with him!

And so at the beginning of the Mass we call to mind all the sins we have committed against neighborly charity in the course of our lives. If we are honest we must admit that we simply cannot count them. "I confess . . . that I have sinned exceedingly in thought, word and deed . . . through my most grievous fault." In the *Introit* we implore forgiveness: "Hear, O Lord, my voice; forsake me not, nor do thou despise me!" Lord, have mercy on us!

In the *Collect* we pray for true love of God, in which of course love of our neighbor is also comprised. For without love of our neighbor there can be no true love of God. "Pour into our hearts the desire for thee, that, loving thee in all things [especially in love of our neighbor] and above all things, we may obtain thy promises." Yes, out of love for God we must love our neighbor, because God so insistently commands it and because our neighbor is His image and likeness, destined like ourselves for the beatific vision in heaven. With great earnestness Peter exhorts us in the *Epistle* to avoid all uncharitableness toward our neighbor, nay more, to feel sympathy and compassion for him. The words are so plain and so easy to understand that no further clarification of them is called for; but to put them into practice, admittedly, can often be hard. In fact the Apostle demands, exactly as did Jesus Himself, that we love even our enemy, to the point of suffering "for justice sake." Sometime, in a quiet hour, away altogether from the holy Mass, we ought to ponder on every word of today's Epistle to see how it is with us in this respect in our daily lives and ask ourselves whether we are true Christians at all.

In the *Gradual* we call beseechingly to God for help. For only His grace can give us strength, in the innumerable occasions and temptations of life, not to offend against neighborly charity. "Behold, O God our protector . . . give ear to the prayers of thy servants!" And in thanksgiving for all past "kingly" victories in this hard struggle let us then sing a joyous Alleluia. "In thy strength, O Lord, the king shall joy."

After the Apostles the Master Himself now comes among us in the *Gospel*. His words are so grave as to force us to a strict examination of our conscience. The Savior refers at the outset to the fact that in the Old Testament it is mainly sinful deeds against our neighbor that are condemned: "Thou shalt not kill." The pharisees seem to have contented themselves with that kind of justice. Jesus supplements and perfects the Old Law: "But I say to you that whosoever is angry with his brother [a sin in thought] shall be in danger of the judgment; and whosoever shall say, Thou fool [a sin in word] shall be in danger of hell fire." Are not these staggering words? Merely by talking and even merely by thinking we can sin grievously against neighborly charity. That is, so to speak, the new fashion that Jesus introduced in regard to the commandment of charity. "A new commandment I give you, that you love one another" even in words and thoughts. Quite independently of our will a whole host of temptations against charity will rise like poisonous fumes from our human nature debased by original sin: envy, jealousy, pleasure at the misfortunes of others, aversion, bitterness, anger, vindictiveness, hatred. So long as we do not consent to such thoughts with our free will no sin is committed. But how easy it is to come to it! And from the thoughts soon come the evil words and deeds.

And now we receive yet another shock from today's teaching of Jesus: He brings the sin against brotherly love into the immediate context of the Mass: "Leave there thy offering before the altar, and go first to be reconciled to thy brother; and then coming, thou shalt offer thy gift!" No one harboring conscious thoughts of dislike or hatred can be a participator in the Holy Sacrifice at which Christ in His love offers up His life even for His enemies. It is an interior contradiction. Let us ask ourselves honestly: do we take these words of Jesus seriously? "Even amongst those who go daily to Mass, how much irritability, quarrelsomeness and disunion we find! How much of the eye for an eye, tooth for a tooth of the Old Testament! Is it not about time that we made a start at fully carrying out the Lord's commandment? Do we wish to have Him challenge us when we appear at the Holy Sacrifice: either — or! Either reconcile yourself with your brother or give up your Mass and your Communion. Neighborly charity is what matters" (Bauer).

We could be saints if only we translated into fact the spirit of the liturgy. Let us make an earnest resolution to do so. The mere resolution is already something great, it is a grace of God. So let us thank the Savior for His teaching: "I will bless the Lord, who hath given me understanding [of the commandment of charity]. . . . He is at my right hand, that I be not moved" (*Offertory hymn*).

Jesus not only teaches, but Himself puts His teachings into practice in the most perfect manner. Here at the *Consecration* He renews His Sacrifice of the Cross where He prayed for His persecutors: "Forgive them, for they know not what they do." He bears in His heart no rancor toward His enemies, but even loves them. If you have anywhere an enemy, go you and do likewise today at the Holy Sacrifice. Pray in this spirit at the *Pater Noster:* "Forgive us our trespasses as we forgive them that trespass against us." At the *Agnus Dei* let us pray for peace among ourselves. In ancient times it was even the custom for the congregation to exchange the kiss of peace at this point.

At the *Communion* we all eat of the same Bread. We feel ourselves to be one family in Christ. Uplifted by this grand community of spirit we pray in conclusion: "One thing I have asked of the Lord; that I may dwell in the house of the Lord all the days of my life." (*Communion hymn.*) It is exactly what Peter said on Mount Thabor: "Lord, it is good to be here!"

SIXTH SUNDAY AFTER PENTECOST

Growth in the New Life

EVERY Sunday Mass is a little Feast of Easter. Even the sprinkling of holy water at the beginning, the *Asperges* (so called from the first word of the ceremony), brings this home to us. It is meant to signify: you should assist at the Holy Sacrifice washed clean of all sins, as clean as after the washing of the soul by baptism. The water that the priest sprinkles on the congregation should remind us of the water of baptism and awaken in us sorrow for our sins: *Miserere mei, Deus!* The psalm *Miserere* of King David is one of the most moving penitential prayers that was ever written. Let us see to it therefore that this introduction to our Sunday Mass is not an empty ceremony! If, during it, we are stirred to true repentance, then its words will be fulfilled: "Sprinkle me with water . . . and I shall be made whiter than snow." It is as newly baptized souls that we should approach the altar.

Every Sunday a little Easter, a renewal in spirit of the baptism received at Easter! This is borne in upon us with very special emphasis by the liturgy of this Sunday's Mass, above all by the two Lessons from Scripture. The *Epistle* tells us: You have received in baptism a new, divine life. The *Gospel,* relating the miraculous multiplication of the loaves, adds: Grow strong in this supernatural life, especially by receiving Holy Communion!

That is also the message of the *Collect:* O God, "grant within us an increase of religion, that thou mayest foster within us what is good [baptism] and zealously guard what thou hast fostered." An excellent paraphrase of the theme of today's Mass.

The far from simple words of the *Epistle* are intended to impress upon our hearts the grandeur of the baptized state. This consists, in a word, in the fact that baptism imparts to us a new, indeed a divine, life. By baptism, according to Paul, we were "planted" in Christ, like the vine branch in the vine. Thenceforth our soul participates in the divine life of Christ, above and beyond its purely natural life. We "walk in newness of life!" What an inconceivable honor for Christians! God unites Himself in a mysterious manner with the life of our soul into one single life. By baptism we are immersed in the divine nature, just as the neophyte was immersed in the waters of the baptismal stream. That is the higher life to which we are admitted. By comparison with it mere natural life can only be called death. "O Jesus, Thou art all my life, without Thee is but death!" Would that we had a livelier consciousness of this dignity of a baptized Christian! Every Sunday, and especially this Sunday, calls it to mind.

And this, to be sure, imposes on us a solemn duty. Not for anything on earth must we deprive ourselves of this supernatural, divine life by mortal sin. We must no longer "serve sin." As Christ after His resurrection "dies no more," so we baptized must fall back no more into the death of sin but must live always with Christ and in Christ. In the words of Paul: Christ "died once; but in that he liveth, he liveth unto God. So do you also reckon that you are dead indeed to sin, but alive unto God."

What a paradise on earth our life would be if, after baptism, we had not to fear relapsing into sin! But the reality is otherwise: we are no longer like Adam in the Garden of Eden, free from evil passions; on the contrary we are very much exposed to them, turned loose as we are into a life of turmoil and struggle. Therefore, in answer to the *Epistle,* we have recourse in the *Gradual* to God, our refuge: "Return O Lord . . . our refuge!" Our confidence thus strengthened we now sing a joyous *Alleluia:* "In thee, O Lord, have I hoped; let me never be confounded!"

In the *Offertory hymn* we continue the same supplication: "Perfect thou my goings in thy paths . . . thou who savest them that trust in thee."

The *Gospel* brings us a truly joyful message: Christ Himself is the bread for our pilgrimage through this life on earth with its many waste and barren stretches. In our day, too, He takes pity on the multitude, lest they faint on their way to heaven. He feeds the hungry in a much more miraculous manner than at that time He fed the four thousand in the desert. "O Jesus, thou art my sustenance, without thee is only want."

That which the *Gospel* narrates now becomes full reality in the Mass in a far higher sense. At that time the miracle was performed through the hands of the Apostles and disciples who at His command distributed the bread; now, at the word of the priest (in the *Consecration*) Jesus becomes present in the bread. His disciples — the priests — distribute it in the *Communion.* He who receives it worthily becomes strong and vigorous; he lives again a new life. By virtue of this food we are strengthened to continue on our journey to heaven. Filled with gratitude for this mysterious bread which itself both "lives and gives life," we rejoice in the *Communion hymn:* "I will sing and recite a psalm to the Lord!"

SEVENTH SUNDAY AFTER PENTECOST

False and True Christianity

TODAY begins a new section in the series of Sundays after Pentecost. Up to now our gaze has still been turned back toward Easter and baptism. From today on the Church exhorts us: bestir yourselves, so that you may bring in rich fruits for the day of the harvest. All around us outside in the world of nature it is now the season of ripening. It depends upon ourselves whether we shall go the way of God's commandments, which is the way of life, or the way of sin, which is the way of death. The liturgy of the Mass for the coming Sundays keeps these two ways constantly before our eyes. We must make up our minds whether we wish to be trees that bring forth good fruit or trees that bring forth no fruit (seventh Sunday); sons of the spirit or sons of the flesh (eighth Sunday); faithful users of grace or squanderers of it (ninth Sunday); proud pharisees or humble publicans (tenth Sunday).

*   *   *

Today's *Introit* is a true hymn of joyous entry. We must picture in our minds the entire congregation of Christians on their way to the parish church: first the children, then the young people and the men and women, and finally the priest with his assistants. From the door of the church we look in at the altar. There we see Christ enthroned in majesty as the Redeemer. We invite the whole world to join with us in paying Him homage and in divine service: "Oh, clap your hands, all ye nations; shout unto God with the voice of joy. For the Lord is most high, he is terrible; he is a great king over all the earth. Glory be to the Father, and to the Son, and to the Holy Ghost. . . ."

In the same joyful mood we then recite that song of praise, the *Gloria*. At the *Collect* we remind ourselves that we are not yet with our majestic God in heaven, but are still only on our pilgrimage toward Him. Therefore we ask imploringly: "Take from us all that is harmful, and give us all those things that will be profitable to us!" In this short prayer all our cares are comprised.

Paul now comes before us as teacher, and the words that he addresses to us in the *Lesson* are certainly very earnest. In sharp outlines he sketches the two opposed classes of men: on the one hand the unbaptized man (the man without Christ); He calls him simply the "servant of sin" — on the other hand the baptized man (the man in Christ), who is the "servant, yea the child of God." Every sentence is pregnant with meaning: "For as you have yielded your members to serve uncleanness and iniquity unto iniquity, so now yield your members to serve justice unto sanctification. Once you were the servants of sin . . . the end of them is death. But now being made free from sin, and become servants to God, you have your fruit unto sanctification, and the end life everlasting . . . in Christ Jesus our Lord." As in the time of the Apostle of the Gentiles, so also today there are still two classes of men. The so-called modern man is not interested in Christ and does not wish to hear of God and His commandments. He wishes to be independent, to be his own lawgiver, to have no one over him. He sees only his own self, his own advantage. Thus he leads a "free life," a slave to all passions. Unwilling to be a servant to God, he is yet willing to be a slave to his own lower nature. But "the end of them is death," the death of the soul, and hereafter the everlasting death in hell. But we Christians are willing to be the servants of God. All our members, body and soul, our mind and our will, belong entirely to God; we surrender ourselves to His holy will and to His commandments. Not merely from fear of punishment, but out of love for the Father in heaven whose children we are. That makes us free and truly happy. And "the fruit thereof is sanctification, and the end life everlasting."

In the *Gradual*, which is the response to this grave Lesson, our Mother the Church exhorts us: "Come, children, hearken to me: I will teach you the fear of the Lord." And now Christ Himself appears, to preach His Gospel to us. Joyfully we greet Him: "Alleluia! Clap your hands all ye nations!"

And lo, in the *Gospel* Jesus continues the stern warning of His Apostle. He, too, though using a different analogy, sets forth two opposed classes of Christians: the first are like an evil tree, that brings forth evil fruit or no fruit; the others are like the good tree that brings forth good fruit. "The evil tree bringeth forth evil fruit": unholy thoughts, desires, words, and actions. Other Christians there are, it is true, who bring forth no evil fruit, but neither do they bring forth good fruit; they are trees with much foliage but no fruit. These are the tepid ones, who are not in earnest in their striving after perfection, who make everything in this life as comfortable as possible for themselves, who do not exert themselves or hold to any kind of rule. The Savior would like to see some fruit! Fruit of contrition and humility, of love of God and our neighbor. Love takes upon itself also sacrifice. Such souls as this Jesus draws close to Himself in holy intimacy. Let us not deceive ourselves: it is not enough that we hold a certificate of baptism, or even that we wear the frock of a priest or the habit of an order. That alone says very little; behind it a sinful heart may be hidden. The Savior Himself has a word for such as these: they are ravening wolves in sheep's clothing, false prophets. And then at the end of His message we have the grave words: "Not everyone that saith to me, 'Lord, Lord,' shall enter into the kingdom of heaven; but he that doth the will of my Father." That is what counts. Only thus are we true Christians, only that is true piety.

And so at today's Mass we offer up the sacrifice of our will entirely to God, praying in the *Offertory hymn:* "As in holocausts of rams and bullocks and as in thousands of fat lambs; let our sacrifice be made in thy sight this day that it may please thee!"

The *Consecration* shows us how Jesus was obedient to the will of the Father even unto death on the cross. He too, as man, was, in relation to the Father, a "servant of God," and it is in those words that the prophet Isaias describes Him. Would that through the renewal of this sacrifice here on the altar today the Savior might grant to us too the grace to be ever obedient to the will of God! It manifests itself to us in the demands of ordered human nature, in the Ten Commandments of God, in the Commandments and Precepts of the Church, in the rules of fasting and abstinence, in the obligation of Sunday Mass and Easter Confession. It manifests itself to us in the duties of our calling, in the duties of a father, a mother, a superior, a subordinate. We must look upon as the will of God all the disagreeable things that befall us in the course of the day: sicknesses, difficult circumstances in our environment, temptations, and interior trials. Only when we accept all these things from the hand of God with entire submission, and still remain serene and cheerful, only then is our holiness genuine and perfect. Then we are truly — as Paul demands of us — servants of God and — as the Savior will have us be — good trees that bring forth abundant fruit. Let us fervently ask this grace of the Savior Himself when He is present within us in Communion: "Incline your ear, make haste to deliver me!" (*Communion hymn.*)

EIGHTH SUNDAY AFTER PENTECOST

Worldly and Heavenly Wisdom

THE first part of the liturgy of today's Mass calls to our mind how rich we are in heavenly treasures. The *Introit* refers to the treasure that we possess in the House of God, our Christian temple: "We have received thy mercy, O God, in the midst of thy temple." In the House of God we were baptized. In it dwells the Son of God Himself with His godhead and manhood, constantly among us, as everywhere on earth as well. He offers Himself up for us in all the churches and chapels in the whole wide world. "According to thy name, O God, so also is thy praise unto the ends of the earth. . . . Great is the Lord, and exceedingly to be praised, in the city of our God, in his holy mountain," that is, in His Church, which Jesus Himself likens to a city on the mountain. In the *Collect* we pray that God may grant us the strength to preserve the grace of baptism and to live in accordance with its prescriptions: "Always to think and do what is right . . . to live according to thy will."

Then, in the *Epistle*, Paul refers to the wonderful supernatural riches that we Christians possess within us. "We are debtors, not to the flesh [not preoccupied with earthly goods and pleasures]. . . . For whoever are led by the Spirit of God [which dwells within us], they are the sons of God. For you have not received the spirit of bondage . . . but the spirit of adoption, whereby we cry: Abba, Father! For the spirit himself giveth testimony to our spirit, that we are the sons of God; and if sons, heirs also, heirs indeed of God, and joint heirs with Christ." In these words Paul portrays the whole greatness of the Christian: he rises above the pleasures of this world, and the Holy Spirit Himself, the greatest gift of all, dwells in his soul. In this way we are transformed into a living jewel of God, yes, children of God. Oh that we might feel ourselves to be such all our days and were able to comprehend this profound mystery! By baptism we are born of God, we share in the nature of God so far as the divine nature can be communicated to a created being. Even now we have a part in the rich life of God, and this gives us a claim to the full possession of God in the life to come. We are heirs of God!

In the *Gradual* we give expression to our childlike trust in the paternal goodness of God: "Be thou unto me, O God, a protector. . . . In thee have I hoped, let me never be confounded!" In the last part of this psalm we acclaim Christ, who now comes to us to preach His gospel: "Alleluia! Great is the Lord, and exceedingly to be praised, Alleluia!"

The second part of the liturgy of the Mass calls on us to be faithful stewards of these great treasures of grace. Thus the Savior, in His *Gospel*, relates the parable of the unjust steward. This man is the prototype of all those for whom earthly riches and worldly happiness are the highest things in this life. He lives, as Paul puts it in the *Epistle*, according to the flesh. In order to make money he does not scruple to defraud. We are told: "The lord commended the unjust steward," that is not to say his dishonesty, but his cunning and shrewdness in having a thought for his future. The meaning of the parable is therefore this: just as this worldly man was provident in his own sphere and according to his own way of thinking, so should you, the children of light, be provident in your stewardship of the heavenly treasures entrusted to you. True, supernatural wisdom, then, consists in this: in appraising earthly things by the yardstick of the Faith; in keeping oneself free from sin, even from venial sin; in detaching oneself (as members of religious orders do by their vow of poverty) from the riches and affairs of this world; in often asking oneself with Aloysius: how does this serve me for eternity; in frequently thinking of God and making acts of devotion to Him, thus laying up for ourselves priceless treasures in heaven "where neither the rust nor moth doth consume"; in being in earnest about obeying the command of Jesus: "Seek first the kingdom of God and his justice, and all these things shall be added unto you." Whoever lives like this brings joy to the Savior, who now appears amongst us at the *Consecration*. And at the *Communion* He offers Himself lovingly to him, so that we actually experience the words of the *Communion hymn:* "Taste and see that the Lord is sweet; blessed is the man who trusts in him!"

NINTH SUNDAY AFTER PENTECOST

The Use and Misuse of Grace

THE liturgy of today's Mass is grave in the extreme. It places us so to speak on the brink of hell, and warns us in both Lessons against neglect of the gracious promptings of God. Salvation or eternal damnation lie open before us, and it is for us to choose between them.

When we enter the church our mood is that of all the Sundays after Pentecost. That is to say, we are conscious on the one hand that by baptism we have been made children of God, but that on the other hand we shall have to face hard struggles in order to preserve our baptismal grace. Therefore at the *Introit* we raise our eyes suppliantly to the picture of Christ over the altar: "The Lord is my helper. . . . Turn back the evils upon mine enemy [Satan] . . . O Lord, my protector."

The *Epistle* then brings out the specific thoughts for this Sunday. Paul warns us Christians not to follow the example of the Jews of the Old Testament. They had received from God graces such as no other people had ever received. On their passage through the Red Sea they had received a baptism and on their way to the promised land had been fed with food from heaven. And yet they fell into the most grievous sins: into intemperance, licentiousness and idolatry. And all this while Moses was praying for them on the mountain and receiving from God the Tables of the Law. "The people sat down to eat and drink, and rose up to play." God permitted that on one day there should fall three and twenty thousand. The Apostle concludes with the stern warning: "All these things happened to them in figure, and they are written for our correction." We Christians are even more deluged with graces by God than were the chosen people of Israel. By baptism we are made children of God, and every day we are fed with the flesh and blood of Christ. But alas, of how many Christians must it also be said: [they] sat down to eat and drink, and [then they] rose up to play." What disdain of the graces of God! They are bent on enjoying life in every way, like the worldly ones, and are hardly distinguishable from the heathen. So we can all take to ourselves the words: "He that thinketh himself to stand, let him take heed lest he fall." But immediately Paul adds the consoling thought: "God is faithful, who will not suffer you to be tempted above that which you are able." Of a certainty, we are weak. Any moment can bring temptation and fall. Baptism and Eucharist give us no guarantee of our ultimate salvation. But if we avail ourselves of God's grace, then we shall stand firm in the midst of temptations.

The *Gradual* seizes upon this comforting thought and thanks God for His protecting graces. "O Lord our Lord, how admirable is thy name in the whole earth! Alleluia!" So we proceed at once to implore of God these wonderful aids of grace: "Deliver me from my enemies, O God," from my lack of deep faith, from my worldliness and all the rest.

The *Gospel* carries the thought of the *Epistle* forward in time. The chosen people of Israel, who in the Old Testament had served false gods, refused to be converted by the countless miracles and exalted teachings of the incarnate Son of God and the chief city, Jerusalem, in particular remained unbelieving almost to a man. Today Jesus weeps over their blindness and obduracy. Soon they will repudiate their Messias and nail Him to the cross. Just as the erring Jews of the Old Testament were punished, so now Jesus foretells a terrible judgment on the unbelieving Jerusalem: "[They shall] beat thee flat to the ground, and thy children who are in thee, and they shall not leave in thee a stone upon a stone, because thou hast not known the time of thy visitation (by grace)." And even today the Savior, at other times so gentle, lays hold of a lash and in holy wrath drives out the desecrators from the temple. A small foretaste of the greater punishment to come. Here too we may apply the words of Paul in the *Epistle:* "These things happened to them in figure and they are written for our correction." How the Savior has literally overwhelmed us with graces, far more than the chosen people! They became a disinherited people, and this could happen to us too. If Jesus were to appear visibly among us at this moment in the church would He not also have reason to weep? To weep over our congregation? To weep over your soul? Would He not perhaps even have reason to prophesy for us too a stern retribution?

The ominous words of Jesus and His weeping have shaken us to the depths of our being. We are resolved to drive out all ungodliness from the temple of our soul, so that the Father, Son, and Holy Spirit may come and make their dwelling therein. We are resolved faithfully to keep God's commandments. Let us today lay this resolution on the sacred paten: "The justices of the Lord [His punishments] are right . . . his judgments sweeter [to me] than honey for thy servant keepeth them" (*Offertory hymn*).

Soon now, at the *Consecration,* comes to us the same Savior who wept over Jerusalem and threatened it with a stern judgment. He does not swing the lash of His anger over us, but instead offers Himself as Victim in atonement for our sins. Grant that He may obtain for us also the grace that we may not overlook "the time of [our] visitation." Let us then fervently beg this grace of the Savior when He unites Himself with us in *Communion.* "Let me never [by a mortal sin] be separated from thee." Rather let me be one with Thee in eternity in accordance with Thy promise: "He that eateth my flesh, abideth in me, and I in him" (*Communion hymn*).

TENTH SUNDAY AFTER PENTECOST

Humility and Pride

Last Sunday the Church made us take a glimpse into hell and warned us: "He that thinketh himself to stand, let him take heed lest he fall!" Today it comforts us with the thought that God takes even the greatest sinner to His heart provided that he is sincere and humble like the publican in today's *Gospel.* So today let us strive, each one of us, to be the humble publican. Whichever of us assists at this Mass with the greatest humility is the one that will take home the greatest share of grace.

I shall therefore recite the *Confiteor* in the conviction that I am the greatest sinner of all those here: *mea maxima culpa,* through my most grievous fault. If God had bestowed on the others here as many graces as He has bestowed on me they would have advanced much further than I toward perfection. That is what the saints thought about themselves. *Kyrie eleison!* Lord have mercy on my miserable sinfulness!

That I have not fallen still deeper is due to the goodness of God. He has given me so much grace and defended me against my enemy the devil. "When I cried to the Lord, he heard my voice" (*Introit*). So, in the future too, I shall place all my trust in the Lord and not in my own strength: "Cast thy care upon the Lord, and he shall sustain thee!"

In the humble spirit of the publican we then repeat the consoling words of the *Collect:* "O God, who dost chiefly manifest thine almighty power in showing pardon and pity. . . ." God must, so to speak, summon up His omnipotence and bestow on us over and over again His all-powerful grace in order to snatch us away from sin and guard us from hell.

In the *Epistle,* with Paul, we attribute all that is good in us entirely to God and His grace. Out of our own purely natural strength we cannot do the smallest thing that is supernaturally good, not even make the acknowledgment that Jesus is God. "No one can say Lord Jesus, but by the Holy Spirit." Independently altogether of any co-operation of ours God distributes His graces and gifts to each of us as He wills. Let us please not overlook that last phrase; let us rather make it our innermost conviction: If we attribute to ourselves the good that is in us then we are still very far away from true humility. Increase in holiness is possible only in a heart that is aware of its own utter powerlessness to make by its own strength even the smallest step in the sphere of the supernatural.

In this conviction we entreat God at the *Gradual* that He may bestow His grace upon us: "Keep me, O Lord, as the apple of thy eye; protect me under the shadow of thy wings." And immediately we add a song of thanks and praise for all the graces we have already received: "Alleluia! A hymn, O God, becometh thee."

In the *Gospel* the Savior takes a concrete case to depict for us pride and humility in prayer in vivid contrast. The pharisee does not really pray at all but presents himself before God in the temple only to boast of his good deeds — and, in themselves, they are in fact good deeds — and to make himself out to be better than the publican. He is so pleased with himself that he does not see his sins at all. It is the same with many a Catholic: away from Confession for a year or even longer he comes into the confessional and can only think of saying: "I have murdered no one, and stolen from no one." A word of self-reproach scarcely crosses his lips. Woe to that proud self-righteousness that sees no sin of its own! The publican, on the other hand, is stricken with shame for his sins and "would not so much as lift up his eyes to heaven." For this — so the Savior assures us — he goes home justified, while the pharisee, who for that matter does not ask for forgiveness, goes away unabsolved. "God resisteth the proud, but to the humble he giveth grace" (1 Pet. 5:5). Humility is the fundamental law of the Christian way of salvation. "The weak of the world [that feel themselves weak] hath God chosen, that he may confound the strong [and great], that no flesh should glory in his sight" (1 Cor. 1:27). Therefore let us not hold ourselves to be better than others. The saints, out of honest conviction, have looked upon themselves as the greatest of sinners.

Conscious of our own sins, "with a humble and contrite heart," we now turn to the altar, placing our sole trust in the grace of God for which we pray in the *Offertory hymn:* "To thee, O Lord, have I lifted up my soul; in thee I put my trust." Acknowledging our own littleness we join our puny sacrifice with the Sacrifice of Christ, and pray: "Receive, O holy Father, this spotless host, which I, thine unworthy servant, do offer unto thee for mine own countless sins, transgressions and failings."

But the most glorious example of humility of all is given to us by the Savior Himself at the *Consecration.* The eternal Son of God, with His transfigured manhood, becomes present under the appearances of bread and wine, to offer Himself up for our sins and then to give Himself to us for food, even to the most wretched sinner. What inconceivable condescension! What infinite love! It is therefore fitting that we should approach the communion rail with the deepest humility. Rightly the Church has us recite today the penitential Psalm 50 (*Miserere*). (Nowadays we find only one verse in the Missal, but formerly the whole psalm was sung.) Thus the thought of the publican brings to a close the Holy Mass. "As the choir sings the *Miserere* the publican receives the pledge of justification. *Ite, missa est* — he goes down into his house justified" (Parsch).

ELEVENTH SUNDAY AFTER PENTECOST

Baptismal Renewal

THE liturgy of today's Mass is wholly imbued with the spirit of Easter, wholly adapted to the renewal of the baptismal experience. That is very striking, for we are already nearly halfway through the twenty-four Sundays after Pentecost. Does the Church mean by this to point out to us with fresh emphasis that all the Sundays after Easter have the same end in view?

On entering the church we are made to realize how lucky we baptized are in fact. We constitute a holy community gathered around the Altar of Sacrifice. This exalted scene is depicted in the *Introit:* "God in his holy place. God makes [baptized] men dwell in unity in his house; it is he who gives power and strength to his people." Let us today recite the *Gloria* — originally sung only at Easter — with hearts full of gratitude and joy for the grace of baptism. Liturgically Easter is the general day of baptism of all Christians, just as it is a general day for the consecration of all churches.

In impressive words the *Collect* calls to mind the unimaginable grandeur of baptismal grace: "O Lord, who out of thy bountiful loving kindness art wont to give beyond the deserts and the prayers of those who humbly pray to thee. . . ." The grace of baptism lifts us up into the supernatural, makes our human nature partake of the nature of God Himself. In baptism God makes our weak flesh the receptacle of divine life. We are no longer mere human beings but are in a sense deified, to use the expression of the Fathers of the Church. To ask for anything so unheard of would seem to us presumption; indeed, of ourselves, it would not enter into our mind that it could happen at all. Would that we might come to a better realization of how great a thing is the sanctifying grace that we receive for the first time in baptism. Supernatural, divine life quickens in us, body and soul, so that we may even communicate to others something of our supernatural life as Jesus Himself has promised: "He who believes in me [through baptism], from within him there shall flow rivers of living water" (Jn. 7:38).

In the *Epistle* Paul proclaims the great message of Easter, on which our entire Faith rests like a house on its foundations. He refers us to several witnesses to whom the risen God had appeared in His new life: to Peter, to all the Apostles together, to five hundred brethren at once, finally also to himself, the chosen Apostle of the Gentiles. And he concludes: "By the grace of God I am what I am, and his grace in me hath not been void." Paul too received grace through baptism, the "life in Jesus Christ" as he calls it, this new Easter life. In him Christ Himself worked the miracle of which the *Gospel* tells, in a highest sense. He opened the inner ear of the former persecutor of the early Christians to the gospel of Jesus, and made his tongue to "speak right," that is to say, He made him the inspired preacher of the word of Jesus in the whole of the then-known world.

In the *Gradual* we rejoice at this great grace that was granted to Saul, and that in a smaller measure is also granted to us in that our life by union with the divine life comes to bloom afresh: "In God hath my heart confided, and I have been helped; and my flesh hath flourished again. And with my will I will give praise to him. Alleluia! Rejoice to God, our helper; sing aloud to the God of Jacob!"

The *Gospel* is a unique and perfect reminder of our baptism. For at our baptism the Savior, through His priest, carried out on us exactly the same ceremonies as He does today on the deaf-mute. The real tragedy in a person thus afflicted is when he has been deaf from birth. Since he can hear nothing he cannot learn to speak even though there is nothing wrong with his tongue. And so a deaf-mute can understand only sign language. With loving condescension and accommodation Jesus employs this language when performing the ceremonies on him. To let him know that He is about to work a miracle on him Jesus looks up to heaven; for it is from there, from God, that the aid will come. Then He puts His finger into the ear of the deaf man as if to open it. He touches the tongue with spittle to convey that He is about to loosen his tongue. The priest performs these very same ceremonies at every baptism. At baptism our inner ear was opened to the words of Jesus, that we might understand their meaning and believe them as commanded by Jesus: "He who has ears to hear, let him hear!" Our mouth was opened to knowledge of the Christian faith, that we might "speak right" not only with our mouth but also by the example of a truly Christian life. Let us then today renew the troth that we have already plighted in baptism, to remain faithful to the word of Christ as the Church preaches it to us.

At the *Consecration* the Savior truly comes to us too, as He once appeared to the five hundred brethren on the mountain and later to Saul on the road to Damascus.

In the *Communion* He confirms anew the miracle of baptism and of today's Gospel: the sacred Host is placed on the tongue. Jesus Himself touches my tongue and says: "Be thou opened, [speak right]!" Then He fills my soul with an overflowing measure of grace, so that my "barns shall be filled with abundance [it is harvest time], and [my] presses shall run over with wine" [*Communion hymn*]. Jesus Himself is the food for the constant growth of our baptismal faith.

In our thanksgiving after Communion let us renew — today's liturgy will suggest it to us — our baptismal vows: Let us once more offer ourselves wholly to Christ. Let us renounce all else beside. Let us dedicate irrevocably to Him all our thought, all our will, all our dealings — day after day.

TWELFTH SUNDAY AFTER PENTECOST

Christ, Our Good Samaritan

THE heading gives the basic thought of the liturgy of today's Mass. In the Gospel we are told: "A certain man went down from Jerusalem to Jericho, and fell among robbers." That man is every one of us, the whole of humanity that had its fall in Adam. The devil was the robber who stripped us of our garment of sanctifying grace and inflicted severe wounds on our nature as well; ever since, it is weak and prone to evil. We can all of us feel this every day. The entire time before Christ passed the wounded man helplessly by. The priests and Levites of the Old Testament were not in a position to give succor to fallen humanity. Certainly the chosen people had been much favored by God. They had the divinely revealed law of Moses, the temple, the daily sacrifice in Jerusalem, the wonderful songs of the psalms, the holy books, and they stood under the special guidance of God. Yet they would have liked to see God — but they saw Him not.

In our day too countless thousands are like the man sunk on the ground, robbed by the devil, and wounded almost to death. Even we ourselves are in constant peril of being set upon by the devouring, destroying devil and losing our garment of sanctifying grace. So today in the *Introit* of the Mass we pray for ourselves and for all poor sinners, with whom we feel ourselves one: "O God, come to my assistance; O Lord, make haste to help me!" Lord, have mercy on me, Christ, have mercy on me, Lord, have mercy on me! "Merciful God, grant, we beseech thee, that we may ever run after thy promises without stumbling" (*Collect*).

And lo, at the earnest pleading of the people of the Old Testament, the Son of God, who from His throne in heaven saw the misery of fallen mankind, mercifully descended from heaven and assumed the form of servant to save us from the clutches of the robber Satan. In Christ, therefore, we place all our trust. In the *Epistle* — otherwise not easy of comprehension — this is most touchingly expressed: "Such confidence we have through Christ towards God . . . who also hath made us fit ministers of the new testament." Certainly the "ministration of death" of the Old Testament was also "glorious." When Moses on the mountain prayed for his people and offered atonement, God allowed Himself to be appeased. And when Moses came down from the mountain "the children of Israel could not steadfastly behold the face of Moses, for the glory of his countenance." In the New Testament it is not a Moses that comes to us, but Christ Himself in all the splendor of His godhead. He is our mediator and our conciliator, our Good Samaritan.

At the Gradual we rejoice over this with thankful hearts: "I will bless the Lord at all times; his praise shall be always in my mouth. In the Lord shall my soul be praised; let the meek hear and rejoice." By day and night our grateful Alleluia ascends to the Savior, our Good Samaritan: "Alleluia! . . . God of my salvation, I have cried in the day and in the night before thee! Alleluia." Blessed are the eyes that behold what we behold! What happiness is ours — to belong to Christ!

The *Offertory hymn* carries on the comparison between the Old and New Testaments begun in the *Epistle*. Moses, the Old Testament mediator between God and His people, prays on the mountain. Speaking of the idolatry of the Israelites God had said to Moses: "My wrath is kindled against them; I will destroy them." Whereupon "Moses prayed in the sight of the Lord his God and said: 'Why, O Lord, is thy indignation enkindled against thy people? Let the anger of thy mind cease: remember Abraham, Isaac, and Jacob, to whom thou didst swear to give a land flowing with milk and honey.' And the Lord was appeased from doing the evil which he had spoken of doing against his people." In the New Testament it is the incarnate Christ, the eternal High Priest, that for us His people presents Himself before the Father and implores forgiveness, immolating Himself for us now in the Mass in an unbloody manner as formerly He did in a bloody manner on Calvary. And so, at the *Secret*, we confidently pray: "Look down, we beseech thee, on the sacrifices which we present at thy holy altar, that they may win pardon for us."

At the *Consecration* the Good Samaritan now appears on the altar in our midst. There He pays the money for our keep. He offers it to the Father in heaven, our eternal host, that He may take care of us and give us all that we need of helping grace. Reverently we bow down before the truly compassionate Samaritan who gives Himself for us with so much love. Filled with pity for our weakness He bends down over us, pours wine into our wounds — His own blood that He shed for us in love and mercy on the cross. Then, in the *Communion*, He pours new life into our soul. Rejoicingly we sing in the *Communion hymn:* "The earth [our soul] shall be filled with the fruit of thy works, O Lord, that thou mayest bring bread out of the earth, and that wine may cheer the heart of man, that he may make the face cheerful with oil; and that bread may strengthen man's heart." And now, strengthened and refreshed, we go forth to our daily life firmly resolved that, after the example of Jesus, we shall be good Samaritans to our fellow men.

THIRTEENTH SUNDAY AFTER PENTECOST

Christ Alone Is Our Salvation

As WE assist at the Mass today let us imagine ourselves to be like the lepers of whom the Gospel tells. What a foul and loathsome disease leprosy is indeed! Its victims were not allowed to mix with other men, but were turned out of the towns and villages, away into the uninhabited caves and plains. If anyone approached they had to shout out from a distance the warning "Unclean," that is to say, do not come near me, I am a leper. Thus the ten lepers too "stood afar off" as Jesus and the multitude approached.

In the prayers at the foot of the altar we acknowledge ourselves to be unclean, through our fault, through our most grievous fault. That is why the priest comes away from the altar, which he had already ascended, to acknowledge "from afar" his own and our sinfulness. The story of the ten lepers goes on: "They lifted up their voice, saying 'Jesus, Master, have mercy on us!' " And so at the *Kyrie* we implore mercy, just as in the *Introit* we called aloud to God: "Look down, O Lord, and forsake not to the end the souls of thy poor; forget not the voices of them that seek thee. Why hast thou cast us off!"

If we wish to be cleansed of our leprosy of sin, then our prayers to Christ must be penetrated with faith in Him as the Son of God, with hope in His goodness and omnipotence, and with dedicated love of Him. We ask for these things in the *Collect:* "Give unto us an increase of faith, hope and charity!" But genuine charity consists in being firmly resolved faithfully to fulfill the will of God in future: "Make us love what thou commandest." One can obey God's commandments out of a sense of duty, or out of fear of punishment. One can also obey them out of love for them. That is the more perfect way. May God assist us to attain it.

The *Epistle* — rather difficult to understand in its full import — aims at awakening in us faith, hope, and love of Christ. Only through Christ can we be cleansed of sin and so enter into heaven. "Neither is there salvation in any other" (Acts 4:12). We must believe in Christ as our Redeemer, and place in Him all our hope. Already to the patriarch Abraham, God had given the promise that mankind would be saved through Christ. The law of the Old Testament had, it is true, warned men against transgressions of the commandments of God, but it had not given the strength for their observance, nor had it cleansed from the leprosy of sins already committed. Only Christ and the grace merited by Him do that in actual fact.

Encouraged by the words of the Apostle — and conscious still of our leprosy of sin — we confidently implore of Christ in the *Gradual:* "Look down, O Lord, remember the reproach of thy servants; thou hast been our refuge, from generation to generation." In the healed lepers of the *Gospel* we recognize our own selves. Many times already has Christ performed on us the miracle of cleansing from sin: in baptism, in the sacrament of penance. The *Gospel* shows that the priests of the Old Testament could indeed certify the fact of leprosy or its cure, but to absolve from sin was beyond their power. Only Christ and, in Him, the priests of the New Testament were to be able to do that.

And so, in the *Offertory hymn,* we proclaim anew that Christ is our All, that in Him alone we place our entire trust. "In thee, O Lord, have I hoped!" Accordingly we place ourselves and all that we are and have in His hands as a sacrificial gift. May He direct the future course of our lives wholly according to His will! "Thou art my God, my times are in thy hands."

The Savior accepts our sacrifice and, in union with His own Sacrifice, offers it up in Mass to the Father in heaven in thanksgiving for all the graces and blessings we have received. In this we join with the tenth leper who, alone of all that had been healed, gave thanks for his healing. "It is truly meet and just, right and availing unto salvation that at all times and at all places we give praise to thee, O holy Lord, everlasting God, through Christ our Lord" (Preface).

At the *Consecration* the same Savior who once made the ten lepers whole enters the "little spots" of our temple, and wipes away with His precious blood the leprosy of our sins. "This is my blood which shall be shed for you unto the remission of sins." Oh that we might have a more lively faith in the redemptive efficacy of the Holy Sacrifice!

In the *Communion* He, the All-clean, gives Himself to us for food, that we may preserve ourselves clean from sin, that our soul may "increase in faith, hope and charity." Gratefully we rejoice in the *Communion hymn:* "Thou hast given us bread from heaven, having in it all that is delicious, and the sweetness of every taste."

FOURTEENTH SUNDAY AFTER PENTECOST

Walk in the Spirit, Full of Trust in the Paternal Goodness of God!

IN OLDEN times this Sunday was called the Sunday of Divine Providence. All the liturgical texts of today's Mass, more or less, are in fact based on God's paternal goodness. It is true that, today also, at the beginning of the Mass we bow our heads in acknowledgment of our sinfulness and cry to the Holy Trinity for mercy. But we do it with complete trust in the infinite mercy of God. Here in the church, where God Himself has taken up His abode, we feel at home.

In this spirit we pray on entering the church (*Introit*): "Behold, O God, our protector, and look on the face of thy anointed [in baptism and confirmation]. For better is one day in thy courts above thousands [outside in the world]." To the true Christian one hour at the Holy Sacrifice of the Mass is the highest good that this world can offer. The thought of his Sunday Mass fills his whole week with joy. There he feels himself transported to heaven, of which our Divine Service on earth is a pale reflection. "How lovely are thy tabernacles, O Lord of Hosts! My soul longeth and fainteth for the courts of the Lord!" In this exalted mood we now sing the *Gloria* as if we were already up there in heaven in the midst of the choirs of angels and saints.

But then we remember that we are still wayfarers in this vale of tears, cast in the midst of a world that is full of temptation. Hence our fervent, childlike, trusting prayer at the *Collect:* "Keep, we beseech thee, O Lord, thy church [our Christian community] with thy perpetual mercy. Without thee the weakness of man is ready to fall; keep him ever by thy help from all things hurtful and guide him to all things profitable to salvation." Yes, the Providence of God knows our weakness. For that very reason it watches over us and shields us from harm.

In the *Epistle* Paul paints in vivid colors the two paths in which men walk: the one, the way of the flesh, the other, the way of the spirit: "The works of the flesh are manifest; which are: fornication, uncleanness, immodesty, luxury, idolatry, witchcrafts, enmities, contentions, emulations, wraths, quarrels, dissensions, sects, envies, murders, drunkenness, revellings, and such like. . . . They who do such things shall not obtain the kingdom of God. But the fruit of the spirit is charity, joy, peace, patience, benignity, goodness, longanimity, mildness, faith, modesty, continency, chastity." From this detailed enumeration of vices and virtues each one of us can examine himself and see whether he walks in the way of the flesh or the spirit. The tragedy is, however, that one and the same human heart, that seemingly is set in the way of the spirit, is yet still susceptible to the perverse inclinations enumerated by Paul. "He that thinketh himself to stand, let him take heed lest he fall!" "No man can serve two masters," we are warned by Jesus in today's Gospel. Yet for all that, how many Christians there are who, on the one hand, would like of course to serve God but, on the other hand, would like to nibble a little at the good things of the world as well! Let us, then, pull ourselves together and dedicate our lives entirely to the Savior without reservation or qualification.

Let us walk bravely in the spirit, not relying on our own strength — we are only too well aware of our frailty — but trusting in God's paternal aid. Thus we sing in the *Gradual:* "It is good to trust in the Lord, rather than to trust in princes." And now, as the Savior approaches to bring us His glad tidings, we hail Him: "Alleluia! Alleluia! Come let us praise the Lord with joy; let us joyfully sing to God our Savior, Alleluia!"

Now Jesus opens His lips and speaks to us truly comforting words as to the tender solicitude of the heavenly Father for us His children. What countless millions of men have received consolation and new courage from today's *Gospel,* even when they were on the point of despair. It is one of the loveliest passages in the whole of the Scriptures: "Be not solicitous, what you shall eat, what you shall put on. Your heavenly Father knoweth that you

have need of all of these things." The words of Jesus are so clear
and plain that no elucidation of them is necessary. We have only to
take them literally, really living as children of God, and then to
trust in the fatherly goodness of God, throwing all our cares on
Him. In desperate situations admittedly it can be hard to find
solace in the exhortation of Jesus: "Be not solicitous! Seek ye first
the kingdom of God!" And yet, humanly regarded, what could have
seemed more hopeless, for example, than the lifework of Christ
when He was expiring on the cross? But He trusted. And God
raised Him up from the dead and through Him gave life to the
whole world down to this day, yes to the end of time. And so before the *Communion* of the Mass we pray: "O Jesus, thou didst by
thy death, through the co-operation of the Holy Ghost, give [new]
life to the world." For the seed must first die, that it may bring forth
fruit. Thus have the saints done, and have seen true miracles
worked in themselves. Whoever gives himself utterly to God, of
him God takes wonderful care. Yet we are of so little faith! We
have been given the same comforting assurance that we have already read in the prophet Isaias: "Can a woman forget her infant?
And if she should forget, yet will I not forget thee" (49:15). Yes,
God's love for us is far greater than the love of a mother for her
infant! And again we read: "You shall be carried at my breast and
on my knees I shall caress you. As one whom the mother caresseth,
so will I comfort you" (46:12). If the almighty God so loves us,
what have we to fear? God is our loving Father! *Credo,* "I believe
in God, the Father Almighty, creator of heaven and earth."

The *Offertory hymn* gives us a further example of the paternal
goodness of God: He has posted angels for our protection: "The
angel of the Lord shall encamp round about them that fear him,
and shall deliver them; O taste and see that the Lord is sweet!"

This infinite love He manifests to us once more at this very moment at today's Mass. At the *Consecration* Jesus comes once more
into our midst. And in the *Communion* He, who clothes the lilies
and feeds the birds, becomes the food of our soul and clothes it
in the exquisite garment of sanctifying grace. Here we see God's
good providence for us at its most touching. And as Jesus takes up
His presence in our heart He repeats the command that He has
addressed to us in today's Gospel: "Seek ye first the kingdom of
God!" (*Communion hymn*). Let us listen to His command!

FIFTEENTH SUNDAY AFTER PENTECOST

Jesus, Who Raiseth the Dead to Life

ON THE second Sunday after Pentecost (p. 101) we referred to the three divisions of the post-Pentecostal season: the Sundays up to the seventh Sunday after Pentecost are a reflection of the Feast of Easter; those of the second period (eighth to fourteenth Sundays) show the baptized person two ways, and urge him to walk in the way of good and shun the way of evil. The remaining Sundays treat of the second coming of Christ. Today, the fifteenth Sunday after Pentecost, is in the nature of a transition: the raising of the dead young man of Naim is already a symbolical prelude to the events of the coming of Christ for the judgment.

How rich in variety, how alive, is the liturgy of each Sunday when one goes over it beforehand with reverent application and then, thus prepared, assists at the Holy Sacrifice! That is the best Sunday meditation! Every Sunday the Savior comes to us in a different guise, to work salvation in us. Today He comes to us as He who raises the dead to life. The *Gospel*, which once again suggests the central thought, tells of the raising up of the dead young man of Naim. The death of a young person is always particularly affecting, even tragic. The widowed mother stands weeping at the bier of her only son. When the Savior sees this He is moved to compassion, and restores the dead young man, alive, to his mother. We can hardly imagine her happiness and her gratitude. But even more shattering than bodily death is, to the true believer, the spiritual death of so many of mankind. Today the Church is the widow who weeps over the state of death of so many of her children. Every mortal sin brings death to the soul. Every deliberate sin, even though venial, is an approach to death and corruption. "He that soweth in his flesh, of the flesh also shall reap corruption" (Gal. 6:8). If in imagination we look out for a moment through the walls of this church into the world outside — how many corpses do we not see wandering through the streets of the towns and villages! Perhaps we may even recognize among them many who are dear to our hearts. This cannot leave us indifferent, since we ourselves are the Church. Let us therefore, now at the Holy Mass where Jesus is about to appear among us, "weep and moan" to Him from the bottom of our hearts, that He may raise our brothers and sisters from the dead, and also that He may bring back to life all that is dead and cold in ourselves and spur us on to new fervor.

Saddened by these thoughts we recite the *Confiteor* at the beginning of the Mass and cry out: Lord, have mercy on us, Christ, have mercy on us! In our prayers, however, we must not always think only of our own selves, as if the rest of mankind were no concern of ours, saying as it were with Cain: "Am I my brother's keeper?" And this should be doubly so at Mass which is essentially a communal sacrifice, offered for all the living and the dead. Today we feel ourselves one with the poor sinners who are in danger of eternal damnation and the horrors of hell. Thus prostrated, we pray in the *Introit:* "Bend down thine ear, O Lord, to me, and hear me; save thy servant. Have mercy on me, O Lord, for I have cried to thee all the day." We may rest assured that if, on this day, all the faithful of good will in the whole world, if we, that is, the Church, implore God and offer up to heaven the blood of Jesus in atonement for poor sinners — God will hear us, and by His grace raise up many of the spiritually dead to a new life.

The greater our love for the poor sinners, the sooner will our prayer be heard. We shall see the fulfillment of that for which we pray in the *Collect:* "Let thy pity, O Lord, continue to cleanse and defend thy church; and because without thee she cannot abide in safety, ever govern her by thy grace."

Through the undeserved grace of God and not by any merit of our own we hope that we are at present in the state of grace and are thus not numbered among the spiritually dead. But here again we must be cautioned: He that thinks himself to live, let him take heed lest he die. How much we too are exposed to sin, and thereby to death and corruption! The *Epistle* reminds us: "Brethren, if we live in the spirit, let us also walk in the spirit!" Before the eyes of all the world we must lead a life of vigorous and living Christianity. If we go through, one by one, the exhortations of the Apostle Paul and examine ourselves honestly on them we shall discover that in ourselves too there is much that is tainted with the corruption of death, in some of us more, in others less. We hanker after empty glory, we provoke one another, we are envious of one another. When we have to correct the faults of others we do not do it in the spirit of charity and meekness. We do not bear one another's burdens. We think ourselves to be something whereas, of ourselves, we are nothing. And so we delude ourselves. "Be not deceived" — the Apostle warns us sternly — "God is not mocked!" Therefore we turn our longing gaze toward Jesus, the restorer of the dead to life, not only out of love for those who are living in mortal sin, but also in awareness of our own frailty and weakness. Jesus has already snatched us from death once before, at our baptism, and perhaps also many times since then in the sacrament of penance. For this we give Him thanks in the *Gradual:* "It is good to give praise to the Lord; and to sing to thy name, O Most High. To show forth thy mercy in the morning [now, at the Holy Mass], and thy truth in the night."

And now in the *Gospel* the Savior appears, to show us by practical demonstration that He does truly raise from the dead. Filled with joy we salute Him: "Alleluia! The Lord (Jesus Christ) is a great God, and a great king over all the earth." And when Jesus then commands: "Young man, I say to thee, arise!" we must take this command as being addressed to us personally. Yes, O my Savior, I will arise from my lukewarmness, to live wholly and only for Thee. What happiness would then be mine! Then would be fulfilled the words of the *Offertory hymn:* "With expectation I have waited for the Lord, and he had regard to me; and he heard my prayer, and he put a new canticle into my mouth, a song to our God!"

And now the reality! At the *Consecration* Jesus, the raiser from the dead, comes down to us, offers Himself once more as Victim, goes to His death, that we may have life! "I am come, that you may have life." In the *Communion* He is the food that nourishes us to a healthy, happy, holy Christian life. "The bread that I will give is my flesh for the life of the world" (*Communion hymn*). And so we go out into the world, there to live a life in God.

SIXTEENTH SUNDAY AFTER PENTECOST

"He That Humbleth Himself Shall Be Exalted"

TODAY there begins already a mild intensification of the motifs of the passion and of the yearning for the second coming of Christ. This corresponds too with the advanced season of the year. The days are becoming shorter, the nights longer. The increasing darkness makes for a somber mood. Hence our supplication of God too takes on a new vehemence, as we shall see presently in the *Introit*.

For the rest, let us look on ourselves today, right through the Mass, as the man in the *Gospel* that was sick of the dropsy, whom Jesus healed. He is a symbol of our puffed-up selves, our pride. So now at the Holy Sacrifice we pray especially for the virtue of humility.

Conscious of our paltriness we implore in the *Introit:* "Have mercy on me, O Lord, for I have cried to thee all the day. . . ." In fact the Church, through its priests, keeps up this cry in the Hours throughout the whole day: "Lord, have mercy on us! Christ have mercy on us!"

The *Gloria* too we recite in a spirit of humility, namely in the deep conviction that God is everything and that before Him we are nothing. "We praise Thee, we adore Thee! Thou only art holy, Thou only art most high!"

The proud man has complete confidence in his own strength. He has no need to pray! But we, for our part, realize that we can produce good works, availing to salvation, only if God supports our efforts with His helping grace: "Let thy grace ever prevent and follow us, and make us continually intent upon good works" (*Collect*). So indolent are we, so weak, so lame even, that God, to awaken our will from its sleep as it were, has to steal a march on us with His grace! God gives the will, and gives the accomplishment. We have no reason, therefore, to brag too much about our good deeds.

Right at the beginning of today's truly admirable *Epistle* Paul gives us an example of genuine humility and selflessness. Before he begins to pray he bends his knee in reverence before our Lord Jesus Christ. Then — he is writing this Epistle from prison — he raises up his chained hands to God in prayer. What does he ask of his people at Ephesus? Their prayers perhaps, that he may be delivered from prison? No, he does not think of himself at all. In a flow of matchless ardor he implores of God, for his faithful, the very highest of all good: a perfect love of God; that the inward man may be strengthened in the Holy Spirit in a holy life of inwardness; that God may dwell in men's hearts. We must at all times feel ourselves to be one with Him, walking in His presence, rooted and founded in the love of God. "That you may be filled unto all the fullness of God." Love of God is the highest of all the virtues; it is like the sun. Thus the Epistle is finely attuned to the season of the year. The days of September and early October are often baked and bathed in the friendly light of the sun. Since the beginning of the ecclesiastical year we too have stood in the sun, which in that context is Christ. We ought by now to be fully ripened, sweet grapes on the vine of Christ, ripe for heaven. The sweetness of the grapes represents warm love of God. But is it so in reality also? If we are humble even we older ones will have to admit that there is in us in fact much that is unripe and unsweetened. We have so little inwardness, and are often so spent and bogged down in earthly cares, that for long periods we forget altogether about God, and perhaps even succumb to sin because we are not yet firmly rooted in the love of God. Then a great longing possesses us so to advance in holiness that when Christ comes to us at death we may have attained perfection.

Yes, the Church knows that one day the time will come when Christ will pass judgment on the whole world, when even the heathens, the unbelievers and the persecutors of Christianity will "fear the name of God" — namely on His second coming at the end of the world. As the *Gradual* prophesies: "The gentiles shall fear thy name, O Lord, and all the kings of the earth thy glory. For the Lord . . . shall be seen in his majesty." There we hear distinctly the tones of the second-coming motif, and next Sunday they will ring out more strongly still. Filled with this vision of the future we now sing a new canticle to the Savior who is "to come in great majesty and glory." "He hath done great things." Great things indeed, especially in baptism, confirmation and the Eucharist!

How moving, now, is the lesson in true humility that the Savior gives us in the Gospel! The bloated victim of the dropsy whom He heals is we ourselves in our swollen arrogance toward our fellow men. "Pride puffeth up." The haughty man is full of presumption, has a great opinion of himself, looks down on others, seeks at all times to push himself forward and to attract attention, must always be the leader. The pharisees in the *Gospel* are a clear example of it. They take it for granted that at all gatherings the first place is theirs as of right. But Jesus gives the counsel: Go, sit down in the last and lowest place. He concludes His exhortation to humility with a maxim that we should all engrave deeply on our minds: "Everyone that exalteth himself shall be humbled, and he that humbleth himself shall be exalted."

In the *Offertory hymn* we implore the help of God against all temptations, in particular against the temptation to pride: "Look down, O Lord, to help me!"

It was at a banquet that Jesus healed the man that was sick of the dropsy, and He followed this up with the sermon on humility. Now at the Eucharistic banquet He does the same for us. At the *Consecration* He is present in our midst though completely hidden under the homely shape of bread. In this He Himself gives us an example of the most perfect humility. Here, truly, Jesus takes the lowest place. And in the *Communion* He humbles Himself still more and unites Himself with the least of all creatures to give Himself to him for food. The *Communion hymn* is deeply affecting. Overwhelmed at the unimaginable condescension of Jesus we bow down before Him and promise to be faithful to Him to death: "O Lord, I will be mindful of thy justice. Thou hast taught me from my youth. Unto old age and grey hairs, forsake me not." All our life long the divine Savior stands before our eyes: in childhood, in youth, in manhood and old age. Always He is the object of our loving devotion. Christ is our All. As He takes up His presence in our hearts today let us keep repeating with St. Thomas: "My God and my All!"

SEVENTEENTH SUNDAY AFTER PENTECOST

Christ Our Lord, We His People

With this Sunday, which as a rule lies in closest proximity to the autumn Ember Days, we enter as it were upon the autumnal season of the Church; the ecclesiastical year is drawing to a close. Outside in the natural world life is dying away. Already, here and there, autumn mist covers the land, and the last of the grain is being brought in. This makes us think of our own end. In the spirit of the Church we prepare ourselves for the second coming of Christ. Liturgically the coming of Jesus at our death and His coming on the last day are treated as one. So in the last Sundays after Pentecost the motif of the second coming is dominant. Nevertheless, in spite of the sobering thought of the judgment, Christian hope is in the foreground, namely the longing for Christ, the Bridegroom of our soul. The bride of Christ, the Church, lifts up her eyes and heart with yearning to her Bridegroom and looks to His coming with silent joy. Today's Mass is as if drenched with this loving yearning. It is a kind of Christ-the-King Mass and its central theme is: Christ, the coming Judge, is our Lord, and we are His people.

❋   ❋   ❋

Already the *Introit* is filled with the thought of Christ, the coming Judge. The early Christians used to adorn their churches with pictures in mosaic over the altar showing Christ enthroned, ruling over the world. As they enter the church in procession all look up to the "majesty of the Lord" (*maiestas Domini*) and sing: "Thou art just, O Lord, and thy judgment is right; deal with thy servant according to thy mercy. Blessed are the undefiled who walk in the law of the Lord."

If we do that, then we have no cause to fear the coming of Christ. And so, in the *Collect*, we pray for such a stainless way of life: "Grant that thy people may escape the defilement of the devil and with a clean mind follow thee, the only God." Only thus are we truly God's people, and only thus is Christ our Lord and King.

In the *Epistle* the Apostle of the Gentiles, too, adjures us to do that which we have just prayed for: "Walk worthy of the vocation [of Christians] in which you are called . . . with patience . . . careful to keep the unity of the spirit in the bond of peace." Here too, as presently in the Gospel, the great commandment of charity is placed in the foreground. In order to implant deep in us observance of the commandment to love our neighbor Paul, in a masterly exposition, even gives the reason why we must love one another from our hearts. It is because, precisely between us Christians, there exists a sevenfold bond of union: We are (1) *one* body; (2) this body is animated by the *one* Holy Spirit; (3) we have *one* goal, namely heaven; (4) we have *one* and the same Lord, Jesus Christ, the Head of the *one* body; (5) *one* and the same Faith; (6) by the *same* sacraments (baptism, the Eucharist, etc.) we are welded into *one* community; (7) we all look up to *one* and the same God the Father in heaven.

If this unity and charity really reigns among us Christians, then we are indeed a "blessed nation, whose God is the Lord!" (*Gradual*). And if the mere unity of God's family on earth has so much that is heart-stirring about it, how wondrously blessed then will be the unity in heaven to which we all look forward with yearning! So the Alleluia becomes a yearning cry of the bride of Christ to her loving Lord: "O Lord, hear my prayer; and let my cry come unto thee. Alleluia!"

Then in the *Gospel* the Savior too speaks of the twofold commandment of charity. He designates love of our neighbor as a main commandment, coming directly after love of God. By it we become one people, Christ's people. More difficult to understand is the second part of the *Gospel*. But one thing immediately strikes us all: Christ here affords us a picture of Himself, seated at the right hand of the Father in heaven; that is to say, the transfigured Christ stands before us, the object of all our longing. As Son of God He is also the Lord of King David, yes of all kings and powers of all ages of the world. At His second coming He will see the enemies of the Church as a footstool at His feet. "All power is given to me in heaven and in earth" (Mt. 28:19). This majestic picture of Christ lights up with consolation the darkness of this earthly life, and, in their afflictions, Christians of all ages look with constant yearning to Christ, "who sitteth at the right hand of the Father."

We do so now ourselves in the *Offertory hymn*. With Daniel, the prophet of captivity, the Church prays that the Lord may allow His countenance to shine upon His Church and upon His people: "Show thy face upon thy sanctuary, and favorably look down upon thy people!"

At the *Consecration* this prayer is answered in a way that we could not expect: the "Majesty of the Lord" appears in full reality among us. Yet not with fear and dread, as later at the judgment, but with grace and mercy. Lovingly He unites Himself with us in the *Communion*. Thus every day we grow in Christ together, to become more and more one single people. He who offers Himself up for us here is He who at His second coming will fill the princes and kings with fear, "who taketh away the spirit of princes; terrible with all the kings of the earth." (*Communion hymn*.) "Blessed is the nation whose God (Christ) is the Lord!" (Ps. 32:12.)

EIGHTEENTH SUNDAY AFTER PENTECOST

Prepare for the Coming of Christ

IT IS autumn outside in the world. The beautiful summer season is at an end. Only a few crops are still to be seen in field or garden. Soon all will be gathered in. The leaves on the trees are already fading and in a short time will fall lifeless to the ground. Today the Church carries these thoughts into the realm of the supernatural. The dying life of the natural world is a reminder for us of our own dying. We Christians are drawing nearer to the coming of Christ, His first coming at our death, and His second coming at the last judgment. This theme of the liturgy of today's Mass is intensified from Sunday to Sunday, culminating in the *Gospel* of the last judgment on the last Sunday after Pentecost. In fact this period of the ecclesiastical year is sometimes called pre-Advent.

This Sunday is like a cry in the dead of the night such as we read of in the parable of the ten virgins: "And at midnight there was a cry made: Behold the bridegroom cometh! Go ye forth to meet him!" (Mt. 25:6.) In fact our Bridegroom, Christ, now comes to us in Mass. Thus our entry into the church today becomes a symbol of our entry into heaven. We have left behind us the discord and unrest of our everyday life with its incessant cares and troubles. Here in the church, on Sunday, a holy peace enfolds us, giving us a foretaste of the eternal Sabbath peace. So at the *Introit* of the Mass we sing: "Give peace, O Lord, to them that patiently wait for thee [Thy coming], that thy prophets [who have promised us this peace] may be found faithful: hear the prayers of thy servant, and of thy people Israel. I rejoiced at the things that were said to me: we shall go into the house of the Lord."

We know of course that into the bridal hall of heaven, of which our church is a symbol, nothing impure may enter. And so we recite with deep contrition the prayers at the foot of the altar and the *Kyrie eleison*. Then, having repented of our misdeeds, we joyfully sing the *Gloria*, that hymn of praise to the Triune God, as if we were already in heaven.

At the *Collect* we beseech God's help that we may so conduct ourselves on earth that we may be found pleasing to the Judge at His coming: "Guide our hearts, O Lord; for without thee we cannot please thee."

The *Epistle* contains a twofold thought: looking back on our past life we thank God for the many graces we have received; looking forward we resolve with God's help to go on courageously on the path to Christ in heaven. Being now at the Ember Days of autumn we give thanks with the Apostle: "Brethren! I give thanks to God always for you, for the grace of God that is given you in Christ Jesus, that in all things you are made rich in him, in all utterance and in all knowledge, as the testimony of Christ was confirmed in you, so that nothing is wanting to you in any grace." Yes, that is how it is. All through our lives God has literally overwhelmed us with His graces: baptism, confirmation, a good upbringing by our parents, the Holy Sacrifice of the Mass and Communion, the divine promptings of every day, the call to the religious life! Today we speak our heartfelt thanks. And to our thanks we add the resolution in the future too to belong entirely to Christ and to prepare ourselves for His coming. "Waiting for the manifestation of our Lord Jesus Christ. Who also will confirm you unto the end without crime, in the day of the coming of our Lord Jesus Christ." Yes,

that is how we wish to spend the rest of our days: freed from the
things of this world and from all undue dependence upon men,
we shall go forward to meet the Lord, resolved that at His coming
we shall be found to be without stain.

So even death gives us no cause for fear; indeed, for us, it means
entry with our Bridegroom, Christ, into the banqueting hall of
heaven. Therefore in the *Gradual* we rejoice: "I rejoiced at all
things that were said to me: we shall go into the house of the
Lord! Let peace be in thy strength, and abundance in thy towers."
And when the Savior now comes to us to preach His Gospel we
hail Him as Christ the King, whose coming at the end of time the
great ones of this world await with fear and trembling while the
good acclaim Him with joy: "Alleluia! The gentiles shall fear thy
name, O Lord; and all the kings of the earth thy glory."

And now we hear in the *Gospel* of the healing of the man that
was sick of the palsy. Today we ourselves are the sick man. The
words that Jesus addressed to him can be taken as addressed to us:
"Be of good heart, thy sins are forgiven thee" and "Take up thy
bed, and go into thy house." The only difference is that at that time
Jesus walked visibly on earth and the sick man prayed for bodily
health. We pray for the health of our soul: that the Savior may
heal it of all palsy so that, refreshed and newly strengthened, we
may hasten to meet our Bridegroom. That is much more important
than the healing of our body. For "what doth it profit a man, if
he gain the whole world (and enjoys bodily health), and suffer
the loss of his own soul?" (Mt. 16:26.) Sunday is always a reminder
of the day of our baptism. We came into the world spiritually
palsied and fettered by sin. In baptism we were freed from the
chains of sin. Since baptism we have sinned again and become
palsied once more. Then the priest, in the name of Jesus, said to
us: "Be of good heart, thy sins are forgiven thee. Arise, and go
thy way." Filled with wonder we thank the Savior, that He should
have given to men that power that belongs to Him alone. It may
be that today we are free from mortal sin — we hope so — and that
we are progressing on our Christian way toward the coming of
Christ. But ever and anon we feel the weakness of our human
nature which drags us down with the dead weight of its evil
impulses. Therefore today we pray to Jesus: deliver me from the
host of passions and evil desires that beset me, that I may rise

above all self-love, all indolence and tepidity, and press onward to God with lighthearted step.

In this spirit let us offer up today the Holy Sacrifice, which is far above the Old-Testament sacrifice of Moses, of which we are told in the *Offertory hymn.* Let us earnestly entreat the Savior, who now stands before us at the *Consecration* as once He stood before the man sick of the palsy: when You come to us in *Communion* free us from the infirmity of our nature, give us new strength to walk in Your way. By daily Communion we keep the oil of love constantly burning in the lamp of our soul, that love with which we go to greet our heavenly Bridegroom. In this way we shall at all times be ready for the moment when the gate of heaven opens and the call goes forth: "Behold, the bridegroom cometh. Go ye forth to meet him!" And when the *Communion hymn* rings out it is for us as if we were already entering into the holy temple of heaven: "Come into his courts; adore ye the Lord in his holy court."

NINETEENTH SUNDAY AFTER PENTECOST

In Expectation of the Heavenly Marriage Feast

TOWARD the end of the ecclesiastical year, ever since the fifteenth Sunday after Pentecost, the Church in its liturgy fills us with thoughts of eternity. Today it does so in the parable of the heavenly marriage feast (*Gospel*): "The kingdom of heaven is like a king who made a marriage for his son." The king is God the Father. He sends His consubstantial, truly kingly Son into this world, that He may draw all men to Himself, unite them with Himself, and lead them to heaven where He celebrates His marriage with them. The betrothal of mankind to Christ, the heavenly Bridegroom, began on His first appearance in this world. In the womb of the all-pure Virgin He assumed our human nature. Ever since He draws us lovingly to Himself, invites us to Himself. He woos every human soul with His grace as a bridegroom woos his bride. "Come to me, all you that labor and are burdened; and I will refresh you!"

He sends His servants, through whom He calls us to Himself: these are the priests of the Church. But alas, a great many pay no heed to His invitation, will have nothing to do with Christ, do not love Him, and do not even believe in Him. Is it not so today also? The great majority of mankind live their lives as if there were no Christ calling men to Him. Many give themselves up to the pleasures of this world or the concerns of everyday life: One "goes his way to his farm" — for him earthly possessions come first; another "goes his way to his business"; he is completely wrapped up in his merchandise, in money. None of them has time to listen to the call of Christ, to His affectionate wooing.

✽   ✽   ✽

But *we* listen to His invitation, which He now addresses to us in the *Introit* of today's Mass: "I am the salvation of the people." How opportunely this voice comes through to us in the perplexity and the great necessity of our time! Would that, after all the frightful things we have gone through, men and nations might at last come to understand that deliverance, salvation, lies only in Christ! More often than in other times Christ calls today to mankind: "I am the salvation of the people. In whatever tribulation they shall cry to me, I will hear them; and I will be their Lord forever." We for our part have already given ear to this call of Christ. We come here in order to enjoy in a mystical manner, here in this house of God, a foretaste of the awaited and longed-for marriage feast in heaven. For the Sacrifice of the Mass is just that: a prefiguration and a promise of the eternal marriage feast that we shall one day partake of in heaven. Let us hope that it will not be with us then as it was in the Gospel: one of the guests had not put on a wedding garment. For this he was cast out of the house of the lord, into the exterior darkness, where there is weeping and gnashing of teeth. If Christ were today to appear visibly in the churches, would He not also find Christians of this sort? These would be those who go, it is true, to their Sunday Mass and perhaps even to Communion, but in a state of mortal sin. Those, therefore, who care nothing for God's commandments, who do not return the love of their loving Bridegroom; for, as Jesus Himself says: "He that loves me will keep my commandments."
Accordingly the liturgy of the Church, today more than ever

(in four places: *Introit, Collect, Communion, Postcommunion*) summons us earnestly to observance of the commandments of God. Already in the *Introit:* "Attend, O my people, to my law; incline your ears to the words of my mouth." And in the *Collect* it implores: "Merciful God, graciously keep us from all harm" — especially from sin, the greatest harm — "that we, being set free both in mind and body, may with ready minds pursue what is thine." But alas, how the devil and our own nature drag us down as with a dead weight!

In the *Epistle* Paul exhorts us: "Be ye renewed in the spirit of your mind, and put on the new man, who according to God is created in justice and holiness of truth." That is in fact our wedding garment of sanctifying grace, through which we become like unto God, a reflection of His holiness. Hence we must avoid all sin, for by sin we lose the wedding garment that we put on in baptism. The Apostle enumerates a variety of sins: lies, anger, theft. These may be taken as representing every other mortal sin as well. But we must be on our guard also against deliberate venial sins in order that we may come to the Sacrifice of the Mass with our wedding garment quite unspotted. These little stains will in any case be wiped out by the *Confiteor* at the beginning of the Mass and by the cry for forgiveness: *Kyrie eleison.*

Then at the *Gradual* we earnestly pray for the grace that from now on we may "put on the new man," that from now on our soul, arrayed in its wedding garment, may become a true likeness of God: "Let my prayer be directed as incense in thy sight." In the *Alleluia* verse we are, as it were, already allowed a glimpse into the celestial banqueting hall and can hear the acclamations of the angels and saints on high: "Give glory to the Lord, declare his deeds!"

The *Offertory hymn* strengthens us in our reliance on the guidance of God, who through all the perils of life accompanies us on our journey to heaven: "If I shall walk in the midst of tribulation, thou wilt quicken me, O Lord; thou wilt stretch forth thy hand, and thy right hand shall save me."

And so, with holy yearning, we silently await the moment when, at the *Consecration,* our host, Jesus Christ, comes to us, His guests at this marriage feast. See, the Bridegroom now appears: go to Him with confiding love. And, at the *Communion,* we celebrate our betrothal with the Bridegroom of our soul. He Himself assures us: "He that eateth my flesh, and drinketh my blood, abideth in me and I in him." To be one with Christ; holy, spiritual, loving union of our soul with the godhead of Christ — that is indeed the whole meaning of every Communion. Already now, by the power of sanctifying grace, we share in the divine nature. And, with every Communion, from Mass to Mass, our soul becomes more and more like unto God, our wedding garment ever more beautiful. Even when the presence in us of the manhood of Jesus comes to an end, He still, by His godhead, remains constantly united with us in bonds of marriage. Only by a mortal sin is this union, by our own act, dissolved. In this wholesome fear of sin we implore our Bridegroom, in the *Communion hymn,* while He is still present in our hearts: "Thou hast commanded thy commandments to be kept most diligently; Oh, that my ways may be directed to keep thy justifications!"

The *Ite missa est* at the end of the Holy Mass then says to us: Go back now to your everyday life, but see that you remain ever united to the Bridegroom, Christ until the day when, at your death, you shall be admitted to the eternal marriage feast in heaven, of which this Mass is a symbol and a pledge.

TWENTIETH SUNDAY AFTER PENTECOST

Far From the Heavenly Home!

TODAY's Mass is extremely impressive and is completely centered on the thought of eternity: we are pilgrims in this vale of tears; banished from Paradise we wander homesick toward our Father's house in heaven. What casts us down beyond all else is our sinfulness. Yet we do not despair. Relying on God's infinite mercy we travel, by His strength, the road of our pilgrimage to heaven. One could call this Sunday the Sunday of Christian Hope. "That is the way of the liturgy of the Church. It knows all about the sins and the guilt of the servants and members of the Church. It acknowledges them and repents of them. But it does not stop short at the sinner. It carries the guilt before the Lord. It confesses it to the Lord and makes of the confession of guilt a hymn of praise to His greatness, justice, holiness and mercy. In faith in His pity and love it awaits the purging of the guilt and the grace that is necessary for inner transformation" (Baur).

✿   ✿   ✿

In this spirit let us recite the *Confiteor* today. And in the same spirit let us sing the *Introit*. "All that thou hast done to us, O Lord, thou hast done in true judgment: because we have sinned against thee. . . . Deal with us according to the multitude of thy mercy." In a spirit of atonement let us bear all the troubles of this life of banishment. *Kyrie, Christe eleison!* In the *Gloria* we see in spirit the transfigured Christ in heaven: "Who takest away the sins of the world, have mercy upon us, receive our prayer!"

At the *Collect* we beg for "pardon and peace." Then, our sins forgiven, our heart is full of peace and holy hope. "Grant to thy faithful people, pardon and peace, that they may both be cleansed from all transgressions and serve thee with a quiet mind."

In the *Epistle* Paul rouses us to a twofold duty: "Redeem the time" — "Give thanks to the Lord!" The days of our earthly life are passing quickly. As we grow older we ask ourselves soberly: What have we done, so far, for eternity? We live too much in the past or the future, too little in the present. Yet the present moment is the only one that we can command. If we do not utilize it, it is gone for ever, unused and unavailing for eternity. Our eternity depends on the use we make, at any give time, of the present moment. Therefore, "brethren, see how you walk circumspectly . . . redeeming the time . . . understanding what is the will of God." At every moment we must do just what God wills of us now. And we must do it well. There are so many things nowadays that entice us to fritter away our time: newspapers, illustrated magazines, radio, cinema, sport, and television. Not that we should not use these things or that we should not have our moments of recreation — but let it be within measure, let there be some control. "Redeeming the time, because the days are evil!" The older we become, the shorter becomes the time still remaining to us, and the more eager we should be — so far as our failing powers allow — to utilize the time for God. First and foremost, in prayer: "Singing and making melody in your hearts to the Lord." We should do this in particular at our Sunday Mass. There, we should "inebriate" ourselves with the Holy Spirit.

And now, at the *Gradual*, we respond to the second call of the Apostle, and sing to God a song of trust: "The eyes of all hope in thee, O Lord, and thou givest them meat in due season." Here we can think of the eucharistic food that we are about to receive later in the Mass; it is a pledge for us of the beatific vision in heaven and of the ineffable rapture with which the soul will then be feasted as with a food. At this thought we feel ourselves already transported to heaven, and we sing: "Alleluia! My heart is ready (to enter into heaven). I will sing and give praise to thee, my glory." "Already now I strike up the chords for the eternal Easter-hymn, the Alleluia" (Parsch).

The *Gospel* takes us back once more into the reality of this vale of tears. A certain ruler begged the Savior to come down to his house and heal his son who lay at the point of death. The ruler had faith in the miraculous power of Jesus, but his faith was incomplete. He thought that for the healing of his son the physical presence of Jesus and the actual touch of His hand were necessary. Jesus makes his faith entire and sends him home with the assurance: "Thy son liveth." So the ruler had to go on his way with only faith to reassure him, and without actually seeing the miracle performed. It is the same with us: we too go through life believing, notwithstanding that we see no signs and wonders. Often our faith in Jesus and in His promises is the only support we have. We cry to the Savior: "Come," "heal us" — but He allows us to wait and even to fall into sin. He wishes to test us, to see whether we nevertheless do not despair but trust in His mercy despite our wretchedness. Deep faith does not waver, even when everything goes wrong. In all circumstances it trusts in the providence of God — without any signs or wonders.

The more we are cast down by all that is earthly, the more firmly we hope in the heaven to come, singing (in the *Offertory hymn*) our nostalgic plaint: "Upon the rivers of Babylon [in the midst of this world of guilt and suffering], there we sit and weep, and remember thee, O Sion." The true Christian feels himself a stranger on this earth and longs, with Paul, "to be released and be with Christ." We ought to feel much more yearning for heaven than we do, much more yearning to be with Christ.

"Come down and heal my son," said the ruler to the Savior. Now, at the *Consecration* and *Communion,* He comes down mercifully to us in reality, comes into our hearts in spite of our failings and our weaknesses. He fulfills His promise: "I am with you all days." "Be thou mindful of thy word . . . in which thou hast given me hope: this hath comforted me in my humiliation" (*Communion hymn*). Mass and Communion are our greatest comfort in this vale of tears. By virtue of this miraculous food we follow bravely in the footsteps of Elias up into the holy mountain, to our eternal home.

TWENTY-FIRST SUNDAY AFTER PENTECOST

Struggle to the End As "a Good Soldier of Christ"!

THE ecclesiastical year is now coming quickly to its close. At this stage Mother Church is fearful lest we may finally weary of the struggle and, at the judgment — of which the *Gospel* treats — may be found wanting. Hence she exhorts us today to fight bravely on to victory as "good soldiers of Christ" (2 Tim. 2:3). In this fight she sees as the enemy, not, as so often before, our weak "flesh and blood" (cf. *Epistle*), but our external enemies, the devil and the godless world who have in fact joined forces against us. Thus the liturgy of today's Mass takes on a dramatic, almost bellicose, character, in contrast with the more lyrical character of the preceding Sundays.

To carry on this struggle we need, above all else, unshakable confidence in the omnipotence of God, our helper in the battle. To this confidence we are heartened by the *Introit.* We repeat, in fact, the prayer that Mardochai sent up against Aman, the enemy of the Israelite people, who wished to destroy them: "All things are in thy power, O Lord . . . Thou art Lord of all."

In the *Collect* we continue to pray for God's help in the struggle against our outside enemies: "Ever keep thy household by thy loving kindness; that by thy protection it may be free from all harm." The almighty God in heaven is our Father, who loves and protects "His family."

The *Epistle* constitutes the strong point of the liturgy of today's Mass. The fiery warrior, Paul, sounds the alarm: To arms! He starts by pointing out the enemy who is threatening to attack us. "Our wrestling is . . . against principalities and powers, against the rulers of the world of this darkness, against the spirits of wickedness in the high places." The very air we breathe is corrupted by the wickedness that holds the world in subjection. The evil world under the domination of the devil — that is our great peril. "The devil, as a roaring lion, goeth about seeking whom he may devour" (1 Pet. 5:8). Then Paul tells us with what weapons we must arm ourselves: "Put you on the armor of God." He even goes into detail and gives a list of all the armor with which a soldier of his day fitted himself out for battle. Paul also explains the spiritual significance of each article. Around the loins a strong girdle — that is conviction of the truth of the teaching of Christ. The breast clad in a coat of mail — that is righteousness, or, theologically expressed, the holiness of sanctifying grace. The head protected by a helmet — that is Christ Himself, the Head of His mystical body. The right hand wields "the sword of the spirit," namely the Word of God in Holy Writ, with which Christ too repulsed the attack of Satan in the desert. The left hand has for protection the "shield of faith," against which the shafts of the devil spend themselves harmlessly. The feet find cover and security because they are shod with the preparation of the gospel of peace. It is for this that we go into battle.

Thus armed, we sing the confident *Gradual*, our battle hymn so to speak, with eyes uplifted to the majesty of the eternal God: "Lord, thou art our refuge. Before the world was formed, from eternity to eternity, thou art God." As Israel then so we now are pursued and harassed by our enemies and are on the point of setting out from the barbarian land of Egypt for the promised land of heaven. For this, in spite of all our afflictions, we sing a joyful Alleluia.

In our struggle we must of course be on our guard against our enemies, Satan and the impious world of men. But we must in charity forgive their offenses and affronts. To this we are exhorted by the Savior in the *Gospel*. He Himself is the king who sits in judgment; and here today the motif of the second coming breaks through at its strongest. If you hope later, at your death and on the last day, to obtain a merciful judgment, then you must now forgive your fellow men, even your enemies, when they do you an injury. In the struggle of Christians neighborly charity is a weapon with which we often disarm the enemy.

Yet another weapon is patience, which is now the theme of the *Offertory hymn:* "There was a man in the land of Hus, whose name was Job. . . ." Satan stripped him of all his substance and afflicted his body with grievous sickness. Yet Job stood firm through all his trials and overcame the devil by his unflinching patience. No matter what suffering came to him, he did not allow himself to be turned from God. To us too, God sometimes sends suffering and struggle, to test us as Job was tested. We must accept them in the spirit that he accepted them, and with the same resignation. "If we have received good things at the hand of the Lord, why should we not receive evil?"

We have much more powerful means to aid us than had Job. For, at the *Consecration* the Savior comes to us, and in *Communion* gives Himself to us, to be our strength in the battle of life. There (in the *Communion hymn*) we renew our prayer for help against the enemies of our salvation, but filled with perfect confidence: "In thy word have I hoped. . . . The wicked have persecuted me: help me, O Lord, my God!" And so we go out from the Mass into the struggle of our daily lives. With God as our guide we feel ourselves strong.

TWENTY-SECOND SUNDAY AFTER PENTECOST

Perfecting Ourselves for the Day of Judgment

ONLY a few Sundays more — and the ecclesiastical year is over, and, with it (in the sense of the liturgy), our life. Then we shall stand in death before the judgment seat of God on "the day of Christ." "*Quid sum miser tunc dicturus*" — What shall guilty I then plead? In this grave and solemn mood, which is to pervade the whole Mass, we enter the church today; and in the *Introit* we moan: "If thou wilt mark iniquities, O Lord; Lord, who shall stand it? . . . Out of the depths I cry to thee." "Lord, have mercy on us; Christ, have mercy on us; Lord, have mercy on us!" At the *Gloria* we adore the sublime majesty of the Triune God and cry out to Christ our future Judge: "Who sittest at the right hand of the Father, have mercy upon us!" He who is to judge us is the Omniscient, to whom even our smallest failings are known; the All-holy, who holds in abhorrence every slightest stain of sin; the Just, who allows no fault to go unpunished. "Thou only art holy, thou only art Lord, thou only, O Jesus Christ, art most high."

If at our death — on the day of judgment — we are to stand perfect before God, so far as this is at all possible for frail mortals to do, we need God's help. For this we pray in the *Collect:* "O God, our refuge and our strength! Thou art the author of all godliness [our striving after perfection]. . . . Grant that what we ask faithfully we may obtain effectually."

In the *Epistle,* Paul the great pastor of souls, speaks to his beloved flock of Philippi — and at the same time to all members of the Christian fold today, ourselves included. They are intimate and tender words. His only care is that all Christians should be perfected in charity, against the coming of Christ as Judge. The Apostle calls this the day of Christ. "Brethren, we are confident in the Lord Jesus, that he who hath begun a good work in you will perfect it unto the day of Christ Jesus . . . I have you in my heart . . . God is my witness, how I long for you all, with the tenderness of Jesus Christ himself. And this I pray, that your charity may more and more abound, . . . that you may be sincere and without offense unto the day of Christ; filled with the fruit of justice, through Jesus Christ, unto the glory and praise of God." What truly golden words! Our greatest care in this earthly life must be to become interiorly better with every day that passes, to travel always along the road to perfection. And the way to do it is this: ever to increase in love of God and of our fellow men. For charity is "the bond of perfection." Paul himself gives us in this Epistle a most beautiful example of it in his tender apostolic love for his Christian congregation.

Let us at this Mass soberly ask ourselves: How do we stand in the matter of love of God? It demands, in the first place, faithful observance of the commandments of God and of the Church. "If you love me, keep my commandments." But this alone would not be that perfection of love that we hope to show on the day of Christ, when He comes for the judgment. Perfect love of God is magnanimous. Before it, earthly things such as riches, sensual pleasures, worldly honors, pale into insignificance and lose all value or meaning. It works only "unto the glory and praise of God," seeks not itself. Hence it bears willingly — if God's providence should send them — sickness and suffering, interior dryness and abandonment, failure and humiliations. It lives gladly in the thought of the ever present God, which brings it interior joy. It prays with Saint Ignatius of Loyola: "O incarnate Son of God, teach me to be generous; teach me to love and serve Thee as Thou deservest; to give and not to count the cost; to fight and not to heed the wounds; to toil and not to seek for rest; to labor and to look for no reward save that of knowing that I do Thy holy will."

Love of our neighbor must go hand in hand with love of God if we are to win our cause before the Judge. Thus the *Gradual* reminds us: "Behold how good and how pleasant it is for brethren to dwell together in unity!" We must not cut ourselves off from our fellows and isolate or immure ourselves from the community, however much we may often be tempted to do so. We must live communally in the family, in the parish, in our circle of friends, in our religious order; live with one another and for one another; pray, and worship, and suffer together, rejoice with the happy, weep with the sorrowful, patiently putting up with each other's failings and weaknesses; in short we must truly love one another. Those who love one another in this way have no need to fear the coming Judge, for it is precisely the manner in which we have practiced charity that He will examine most searchingly. Thus we can with humble confidence await the day of Christ. "Alleluia! They that fear the Lord, let them hope in him: he is their helper and protector. Alleluia!"

And just as in our little circle we practice charity among our equals, so also must we fulfill our duty toward our superiors if we are to pass the test on the day of judgment; toward both our civil and our ecclesiastical superiors. That is what Jesus Himself enjoins on us in the *Gospel:* "Render to Caesar the things that are Caesar's, and to God the things that are God's." We must play our part in the building up of the state and the fatherland so that material prosperity may reign in the land. But still more in the advancement of the kingdom of God, in the deepening of Christianity.

And behold: At the *Consecration* Christ, our Judge to come, appears on the altar, hidden in the sacrament it is true, but still wholly the same. Would that at that moment we might find adequate words! "Remember me, O Lord, thou who rulest above all power, and give a well-ordered speech in my mouth, that my words may be pleasing in the sight of the prince" — as we reverently pray with Queen Esther in the *Offertory hymn.*

The *Communion* is an anticipation of the judgment. Today the Lord comes to us as friend; later He will come as Judge. Let us receive Him into our hearts with the greatest awe, but also with the most fervent love, and pray to Him: "O Jesus, be not to me a judge, but a Savior!" Whoever seeks always to serve the Savior faithfully has no need to fear the "day of Christ." Of this we are assured in the *Communion hymn:* "To thee have I cried, and thou hast heard me, O God; Oh, incline thine ear unto me [on the day of judgment] and hear my prayer [for Thy gracious mercy]."

TWENTY-THIRD SUNDAY AFTER PENTECOST

Homesick for Heaven

THE liturgy of the concluding Sundays of the ecclesiastical year breathes the spirit of primitive Christianity. The Christians of those early times thought that they themselves perhaps might witness the return of Christ to this world for the judgment; the Savior had not foretold any specific time. So they lived in the constant expectation that Christ would come and take them home with Him to heaven. Little wonder that in that age of bloody persecution there grew up a heroic race of martyrs and a race of virgins of austere and fragrant purity. Would that we Christians of our day might live more in this expectation of the coming of Christ the Judge!

He may indeed come suddenly like a thief in the night – the Savior Himself used that simile. We ought to have a greater nostalgia for heaven. The liturgy of the Mass of this Sunday brings this thought particularly before our minds; in fact it hardly speaks of anything else.

Already in the *Introit* we meet with it: "The Lord saith: 'I think thoughts of peace, and not of affliction. You shall call upon me, and I will hear you; and I will bring back your captivity from all places.' Lord, thou hast blessed thy land: thou hast turned away the captivity of Jacob." When Christ appears at the judgment He will bring home His own to Him in heaven. "Come, ye blessed of the Father, receive you the kingdom that has been prepared for you." And Christ conducts His faithful on high to the Father, people "from all places," from all regions and all times. The homecoming of the people of Israel, of the stock of Jacob, from their banishment in Babylon is a small thing in comparison. God, the Lord, is good, and thinks only thoughts of peace. He desires that all men shall win eternal salvation and happiness.

But, as yet, we are still in exile in this vale of tears, in captivity. The chains that hold us down are sins and the bonds, light or heavy, that still bind us to purely earthly things. Oh, that we might be freed for ever from all that is not God! For this we pray in the *Collect:* "Absolve, O Lord, we beseech thee, thy people from their offenses; that through thy bountiful goodness we may be freed from the bonds of those sins which through our frailty we have committed."

And now once more Paul appears before us, this time with chains on his hands. For he wrote the *Epistle* to the Philippians from the prison in Rome. But he is not troubled about the chains that bind his hands as he writes. What grieves him, the zealous pastor, and even forces the tears to his eyes, is the knowledge that so many men – even Christians – spend their lives in the chains of sin and give no thought to another world: "Brethren, many walk, of whom I have told you often [and now tell you weeping], that they are enemies of the cross of Christ; whose end is destruction, whose God is their belly, and whose glory is their shame; who mind earthly things. But our conversation is in heaven. [We desire while still on earth to live as if we were already in the next world]; from whence also [down from heaven] we look for the Savior, our

Lord Jesus Christ [to His coming for the judgment], who will reform the body of our lowness, made like to the body of his glory." In conclusion, with fatherly anxiety, he bids his Christians: "Stand fast in the Lord, my dearly beloved!"

If we live, not "for our belly" like the enemies of Christ, but with our thoughts ever turned on eternity, on heaven, then we can with full confidence answer the Epistle with the joyful words of the *Gradual* as if we had already been assumed into heaven with Christ: "Thou hast delivered us, O Lord, from them that afflict us. . . . In God we will glory all the day, and in thy name we will give praise for ever. Alleluia." But then we remind ourselves that we are still here below, pilgrims in a foreign land, and in our home-sickness we pray: "Out of the depths I have cried to thee, O Lord: Lord, hear my prayer!" And presently in the *Offertory hymn* we repeat this same nostalgic prayer. It is a hymn of yearning for the second coming of Christ and for our homecoming to the eternal home of our Father.

And now, in answer to our longing prayer, Christ appears in the *Gospel* and brings us — not by words, but by miraculous deeds — true tidings of great joy. Just as He healed the sick woman, who trustingly touched the hem of His garment, so too He heals us from the sinful urgings of our weak nature. "Be of good heart, daughter, thy faith hath made thee whole" — He says this also to us at this moment. And as He awakened the daughter of Jairus from death to life, so, at His coming at the judgment, will He awaken our body and — as Paul says in the *Epistle* — make it like to the body of His glory.

Yes, it is as if the Savior, in His goodness, could not wait for the day of His second coming to work this miracle in us. So already today, He appears here on the altar at the *Consecration.* There He immolates Himself for us to the Father as expiatory Victim. Well may we say that He has for us "thoughts of peace, and not of affliction."

And in *Communion* He unites Himself with us most interiorly and so gives us a pledge of the resurrection of our body on the last day. "If I shall touch only his garment, I shall be healed," the heathen woman, profoundly believing, said to herself. We Christians must not allow ourselves to be put to shame by her faith. We know that at Communion we not merely touch the hem of the garment of Jesus, but receive Himself, with His godhead and His manhood, within ourselves. With what trust this fills our hearts! He who heard and granted the prayer of the administrator of the synagogue and the mute longing of the sick woman will also hear our prayer that we make to Him when we receive Him in our breast, and will grant it. For He has explicitly promised: "Amen I say to you, whatsoever you ask when you pray, believe that you shall receive, and it shall be done unto you" (*Communion hymn*).

FIFTH (PASSED OVER) SUNDAY
AFTER THE EPIPHANY*

"Suffer Both the Wheat and the Cockle to Grow Until the Harvest!"

THE Sundays after the Epiphany of the Lord which no longer came into the Christmas cycle because of the early falling of Septuagesima are now made up at the end of the ecclesiastical year. (These are for the most part the fifth and the sixth Sundays.) They are well suited to the end season, for in today's *Gospel* Jesus speaks of the cockle which at His second coming will be cast into the fires of hell, and of the wheat that will be gathered into the heavenly granary. That is the theme of the liturgy of today's Mass: wheat and cockle on the tilled field of our soul and on the tilled field of the Church.

Outside in the open country the tilled land depends for its fruitfulness on rain and sunshine from above. Likewise in the field of our soul and of the Church the wheat can thrive only if the heavenly Father allows His grace to descend. "Therefore, neither he that planteth is anything, nor he that watereth; but God that giveth the increase" (1 Cor. 3:7). For this grace we pray in the *Collect:* "Keep, we beseech thee, O Lord, thy household in thy continual mercy; that as it leans only upon the hope of thy heavenly

* This Mass is said on the twenty-fourth Sunday after Pentecost in years when there are twenty-six Sundays after Pentecost.

grace, so it may ever be defended by thy protection." Defend us also against Satan and his evil seed!

In the *Epistle* Paul shows us the tilled field of a Christian soul, where only wheat takes root, in particular the virtue of neighborly charity. "Put ye on . . . the soul of mercy, benignity, humility, modesty, patience: bearing with one another and forgiving one another. . . . But above all these things, have charity. . . . wherein also you are called in one body." Of love of God the Apostle has this to say: "Let the word of Christ dwell in you abundantly . . . in psalms, . . . singing in grace in your hearts to God. All whatsoever you do in word or in work, do all in the name of the Lord Jesus Christ." All our daily work should be inspired by the ideal: all for God. Then truly we should yield an abundant harvest on the day of judgment. That is the goal at which we have to aim.

In the *Gradual* we comply at once with the call to the praise of God and sing: "Thou hast delivered us, O Lord, [through the work of Thy redemption]. . . . In God we will glory all the day; and in thy name we will give praise for ever. Alleluia!" On the other hand when we meditate on the *Epistle* we have frankly to acknowledge that side by side with many virtues there is in our soul no small luxuriance of cockle. Humbly, therefore, we implore: "Out of the depths I cry to thee, O Lord; Lord, hear my prayer," show me Thy indulgence. This same supplication we make yet a second time in the *Offertory hymn*.

And now in the *Gospel* the Savior relates the parable of the cockle among the wheat. The servants wanted to root up the cockle on the spot. But God, the Owner of the field, gives the order: "Let both grow until the harvest. Then I will say to the reapers: gather up first the cockle, and bind it into bundles to burn, but the wheat gather ye into my barn." As long as the world endures freedom is allowed to the devil. He sows cockle in the garden of the Church of Christ. And unfortunately we have also to behold cockle growing, and growing rampant, in individual human souls, in parish congregations and dioceses, and even in religious communities. How many deplorable examples of this do we not find in the history of the Church! How much apostasy, betrayal, immorality, false piety! Should we not set to and root it out? "No, suffer both to grow." If we tried to root out the cockle in the wheat field we should trample down and destroy the ears of wheat. Let the cockle remain! This will sorely grieve the good. But the confrontation with evil will serve them as a frightening example and will afford many opportunities for the constant practice of virtue. Until the end of time the Christian community will be a Church of saints and sinners. There will never be a Church of nothing but the sainted, the pure and the anointed. Indeed it was for the saving of sinners that Christ set up His Church. In the tilled field of Christ cockle can be transformed into wheat. The zealots would like nothing better than to call down fire from heaven to destroy all sinners and cast them into hell. We see only the transiency of time, but God the Eternal can wait for the conversion of the wicked. None, of course, can escape His eventual judgment. And so He suffers both to grow — until the end of time.

Each of us can further apply this parable to the field of his own soul. Already in baptism God planted good seed in our soul: sanctifying grace and the various concomitant virtues and good dispositions. Every day He nourishes these supernatural germs and forces by means of the Holy Sacrifice, Communion, and the many promptings of His grace. Every week, perhaps, you make your Confession, every month your act of spiritual renewal, every year your retreat. Why is it, then, that there is so much cockle in the soul? Even if there be no actual mortal sin, there are certainly many deliberate venial ones, many semi-deliberate ones of thoughtlessness, many temperamental lapses. And still it would be the fondest dream of all virtuous souls to be and to remain absolutely free from all that is disordered; that never and nowhere should the smallest fault occur; that even the slightest trace of cockle should not be found. Yet here too the words of the Savior apply: "Suffer both" — wheat and cockle — "to grow." This is not to say that we must not resist the evil in us. But God in His providence has so ordained that it is beyond our power to eradicate the shoots of evil inclinations and desires. They will therefore be for us over and over again the occasion of faults and sins. We must learn to bear these weaknesses and frailties of our human nature in patience and humility and not to lose heart over them. What purpose does the cockle serve? It serves as a constant reminder of our own wretchedness and thus gives us understanding for the weaknesses of our fellows. It serves to prevent us from ever getting puffed up with pride and to make us always feel ourselves small in the eyes of God and men. It serves to make us turn trustingly to the compassionate Heart of Jesus for pardon for our sins.

Let us also implore His mercy when at the *Consecration* He pleads with the Father on our behalf for forgiveness. Then, when our hearts are once more cleansed of our daily misdeeds, He descends at the *Communion* joyfully into the soil of our soul as the heavenly Wheat Seed. Let us at that moment beseech Him so to strengthen us that we may remain free at least from consciously committed and fully deliberate sin. Then may the promise of Jesus be fulfilled, of which the *Communion hymn* gives word: Whatsoever you ask when you pray, believe that you shall receive, and it shall be done unto you.

SIXTH (PASSED OVER) SUNDAY AFTER THE EPIPHANY

Perfected in Christ

THE ecclesiastical year now stands immediately before its close. Hence the liturgy of the Mass of the penultimate Sunday presents to our eyes the realization of the kingdom of God on earth. Outwardly it has become a mighty tree; inwardly, in a sort, it leavens the whole of mankind like yeast. To what extent have we ourselves now been perfected in Christ?

Are we already in such a spiritual state that Christ, when presently He comes for the judgment, can gently say to us (*Introit*): "I think thoughts of peace . . . I will bring back your captivity from all places." Truly, in the ecclesiastical year that is just ending Christ Himself has once more done everything to ensure that we might today stand perfected before Him, "freed" from all sinfulness and godlessness. — Has our soul really come that far? Lord, have mercy on us! Christ, have mercy on us!

Conscious of our deficiencies we pray, in the *Collect,* for perfection: "Grant that, ever fixing our thoughts on reasonable things, we may both in our words and works do what is pleasing in thy sight." Yes, if in our thoughts and words and actions we always had before our eyes the will of God, then we should indeed be perfect Christians. We should be able to say, with Christ: "My meat is to do the will of him that sent me" (Jn. 4:34).

In the *Epistle* Paul represents his Thessalonians to us as a perfect Christian community. The Apostle had brought them the wheat seed of the Gospel as the "power and fullness of God." They had received it with faith and had allowed it to work in them despite every persecution. And so the three divine virtues blossomed in them. "Brethren: we give thanks to God always for you all, being mindful of the work of your faith, and labor, and charity, and of the enduring of the hope of our Lord Jesus Christ." For this reason he calls them the "elect." By their exemplary Christian virtues they came to be for other communities a powerful leaven: "You were made a pattern to all that believe. From you was spread abroad the word of the Lord. . . . In every place your faith is gone forth." — Is our parish also a model Christian community, perfected in Christ? How is it with us in the matter of our faith, our hope, our charity?

A Christian community of the pattern of the Thessalonians can conscientiously recite the *Gradual:* "Thou hast delivered us, O Lord, from them that afflict us. . . . In thy name we will give praise for ever. Alleluia!" Nevertheless, in expectation of the coming of the Lord, who will examine us on how we stand as regards perfection, our hymn of joy changes suddenly into the troubled *De profundis:* "Out of the depths I cry to thee, O Lord; Lord, hear my prayer!"

And now, in the *Gospel,* Christ Himself appears before us and expounds a twofold parable of profound import. "The kingdom of heaven is like to a mustard seed. . . . When it is grown up, it becometh a tree. The kingdom of heaven is like to leaven, which leavened three measures of meal." That is our Holy Church: a mustard seed by reason of its propagation, and a leaven by reason of its spiritual potency. Christ Himself was the mustard seed, quite insignificant at His death, crushed as it were, consigned to the earth of Jerusalem. Yet how swiftly the insignificant apostolic community spread itself forth! Over the whole of Palestine, Asia Minor, Egypt, over the vast Roman Empire. And today it is a tree whose roots extend over the entire world. In the realm of the spirit Christianity is like to a leaven. The teaching of Christ, with its exalted precepts, leavens its adherents scattered far and wide over the earth. Countless men of all ages have been penetrated with the truth of Christ, detaching themselves from earthly things and dedicating themselves wholly to God. "The fruit of the Spirit is charity, joy, peace, patience, benignity, goodness, longanimity. And they that are Christ's have crucified their flesh, with the vices and concupiscences" (Gal. 5:22, 24). And we? How far are we penetrated by the leaven of the teachings of Christ? The leaven is the divine life in us, the "new creature" (Gal. 6:15). We would then by our example ourselves become a mustard seed and make an immense contribution to the spreading of Christianity in our immediate circle.

(*Consecration* and *Communion*.) "Daily we experience the transforming power of the Holy Sacrifice. Daily His Body is sown in us as seed. God acts upon us through His sacraments (divine life). In manifold ways the power of the Lord operates through the Sacred Species; all we have to do is not to resist. They are unobtrusive, a mustard seed, a leaven. But their effect is great beyond measure: they transfigure the world" (Lohr). In the end comes the day when we can say: "I live, now not I; but Christ liveth in me" (Gal. 2:20).

Let us pray perseveringly that when in due course our life on earth is over we may be able to appear before the Judge as perfected as possible. God will hear such a prayer; He has promised to do so: "Amen I say to you, . . . believe that you shall receive, and it shall be done unto you" (*Communion hymn*).

TWENTY-FOURTH AND LAST SUNDAY AFTER PENTECOST

The Son of Man Will "Come With Much Power and Majesty"!

IN THE ecclesiastical year which closes today we have lived through the redemptive life of Jesus: incarnation, passion, death, resurrection, and ascension, the sending of the Holy Spirit, the foundation and growth of the Church, its union with Christ, its Head, our

Redeemer and Deliverer. Through these mystical feasts we have been filled with His divine life. Only one thing is lacking: our own ascension into heaven, the homecoming of the Church to the Father through Christ. On today, the Last Sunday after Pentecost, the liturgy of the Church allows this last act of the drama of the redemption to be enacted before our eyes. The Last Sunday carries us into the immediate vicinity of the first judgment, nay makes us live through, in anticipation, the "day of Christ." Truly a wonderful spectacle!

The prayers at the foot of the altar are the beginning of the judgment. At the *Confiteor* we stand before Christ, the Judge. "*Judica me, Deus,* Judge me, O God," is the opening prayer. Christ appears "in much power and majesty," surrounded by all the angels and saints. It is a court scene. We are charged as evildoers and we plead guilty: "Through my fault, through my most grievous fault." Nevertheless we call upon the saints, with Mary at their head, to be our advocates: "to pray to the Lord, our God, for us." But of the Lord Himself we implore: *Christe eleison!* Divine Judge, be merciful to us!

To our contrite acknowledgment of our guilt — already blotted out by our Confession — the Judge Himself now replies in the *Introit:* "I think [for you, my faithful] thoughts of peace, and not of affliction . . . I will bring back your captivity from all places." The earliest Christians did not fear this day, but sighed for the second coming of Christ. So deep was their faith, so strong their Christian hope. Thus should it be likewise with the Christians of today. For all who remain true to Christ in this life, before the eyes of the world, the day of the last judgment is the day of their entry with Christ into heaven, a yearned-for day, on which we take part in the triumph of our King over the ungodly world.

And so, already, here and now, we feel ourselves transported into the company of those who will then stand at the right hand of God. In union with them and the angels and saints who throng about the Judge we sing the *Gloria:* "We praise thee, we bless thee, we adore thee. . . . Thou only art holy, thou only art Lord, thou only art most high: Jesus Christ, together with the Holy Ghost, in the glory of the Father."

With its stormy *Excita* (stir up) the *Collect* already sounds like an Advent prayer; and in fact our gaze is now directed toward the new ecclesiastical year. The right resolution, at the close of the year, is to make even better use of the year of grace that is to follow. "Stir up the (sluggish) will of thy faithful, that they may more earnestly" serve thee and "more abundantly receive the healing gifts of thy mercy."

This request is repeated in the *Epistle*, which shows how our zeal in the service of God should manifest itself: above all, in the "clear knowledge of the will of God" (and in readiness to fulfill it) "that you may walk worthy of God, in all things pleasing." The virtues of "patience and long-suffering" are singled out for special mention. Thus we prepare ourselves worthily for the coming of Christ for the judgment. Now already, ever since at baptism He received us into His kingdom, the Church, He has chosen us out from many, and on the last day He will choose us out once more for heaven. Then shall we be made partakers "of the lot of the saints in light"; then shall we be "delivered from the power of darkness and translated into the kingdom of the Son of his love." For this let us joyfully "give thanks to God the Father."

In answer to the words of the Apostle we do this jubilantly in the *Gradual:* "Thou hast delivered us, O Lord, from them that afflict us. . . . In God we will glory all the day, and in thy name we will give praise for ever." Joyfully we add the Alleluia which, when Christ has gathered us up to our heavenly home, "we shall soon be singing in bliss in the streets of the celestial Sion" (Parsch). But, for the present, our life on earth is not yet over; we are definitely not yet absolutely certain of our salvation. We do not know whether we shall always remain true to God and whether, accordingly, at the last judgment, we shall stand at the right hand of the Judge or at the left. So today we fervently implore of the Savior our deliverance at the last judgment: "Out of the depths I cry to thee, O Lord; Lord, hear my prayer."

In the *Gospel* we are shown the second coming of Christ for the judgment of the world. The Savior Himself describes the whole scene for us in clear and solemn words which every year grip us anew. He wishes to warn us, even in the midst of the darkness of this earthly life, to walk in the light of the Day of Christ for which we yearn. For the prophecy of Jesus as to the desolation of that day should fill us, not merely with wholesome fear, but also with happy courage. It is for us the inviting words of the Judge are intended: "Come, ye blessed of my Father, possess you the kingdom prepared for you from the foundation of the world." In sanctifying grace we carry even now in our souls the title deeds to this glorious kingdom of indescribable bliss.

The *Credo*, too, bears today a special complexion. On November 1, 1950, on the occasion of the promulgation of the dogma of the Assumption of Our Lady into Heaven, there gathered together about a million Catholics in the vast Square of St. Peter's in Rome. When, with one voice, they sang the *Credo* it was like the mighty roar of a surging sea. At the last judgment — we may reasonably imagine — it will be milliards of the elect that will be singing the *Credo* in unison. All the more mightily will its concluding words ring out because they are there and then being brought to fulfillment: I believe "in the resurrection of the body and in life everlasting."

The day of the coming of Christ for the judgment will be for us merely the shining manifestation of the reality that we experience in faith today at the Holy Mass. At the *Consecration* the divine Judge descends, not with power and majesty in the clouds of heaven, but hidden behind the little film of the Sacred Host. In the *Communion* He offers Himself as the pledge of the resurrection of our body. "He that eateth my flesh, I will raise him up in the last day" (Jn. 6:55). When, at that solemn moment, the Savior is present in our breast, let us humbly adore Him as our future Judge and from our hearts implore: "Jesus, be not to me a judge, but a Savior!" And then it may well be as if we heard the answering promise of Jesus: "Amen I say to you, whatsoever you ask when you pray, it shall be done unto you" (*Communion hymn*).

FEAST OF THE DEDICATION OF A CHURCH

"This Day Is Salvation Come to This House!"

EVERY year each parish community commemorates with joy and gratitude to God the anniversary of the consecration of its church, the dwelling place and mercy seat of God in our midst.

Today — in the spirit of the liturgy — let us imagine as we enter our parish church that it is just now that it is being dedicated. With the bishop we approach to assist for the first time here at the Holy Sacrifice. This symbolizes the entry of Christ Himself into this holy abode. Thereby it becomes a place that we should enter only with awe; but also it becomes a fragment of heaven on earth. These two feelings, religious awe and holy joy, find expression in the *Introit:* "Terrible is this place: it is the house of God, and the gate of heaven the court of God. How lovely are thy tabernacles, O Lord of hosts!"

Here the Son of God dwells both as man and God — in the tabernacle (tent) — here alone He is near to us as man. Here He consummates daily His sublime Sacrifice. Here He draws us into His sheltering love. Here we tell Him all our cares. Here sooner than anywhere else our prayer finds hearing. So in the *Collect* we implore: "Grant that whosoever shall enter into this holy temple to ask good things from thee may receive with joy whatever he shall ask." If the promise of this was made by God to King Solomon in regard to the temple of the Old Testament how much the more must this promise hold good for the Christian Church!: "The Lord said: My eyes also shall be open, and my ears attentive to the prayer of him that shall pray in this place" (2 Par. 7:15).

The *Lesson* now gives a moving account from the Apocalypse of the greatness and majesty of the house of God: At the dedication of our church it is as if a piece of heaven had come down into this house. There now God dwells in our midst; we have become His people. There, attentive to our prayers, He wipes away all our tears; death is no more, nor mourning. Here He accomplishes our deliverance from our sins and from all evil. How many pious Chris-

173

tians have affirmed that when assisting at a beautiful service in church they have felt themselves to be in heaven!

In the *Gradual* — meditating on what we have heard in the Epistle — we give expression to our joyful confidence: "This place was made by God, a priceless covenant. O God, before whom stands [here] the choir of angels, graciously hear the prayers of thy servants!" However, it is not only in order to ask, that we are met together in the church, but also to adore God and praise Him: "Alleluia! I will worship toward thy holy temple, and I will give glory to thy name."

On the day of the dedication of our church we find ourselves exactly in the position of the publican Zachaeus of whom the *Gospel* speaks. Into "our house" — this church belongs to us all — the Savior enters, and dwells among us, and shares with us the entire fullness of His grace. "This day is salvation come to this house!" Oh, that we too might receive Jesus with the same joy, the same humility and the same spirit of self-sacrifice as the publican when he said: "behold, Lord, the half of my goods I give to the poor, and if I have wronged any man of anything, I restore him fourfold." So powerfully had the gracious presence of Jesus worked on him that the heart of Zachaeus underwent a complete transformation. Time and again we see the same thing happen in this House of God to all who are of good will.

In the *Offertory hymn* we ask, for ourselves and all here present, that we may be granted this good will, this singleness of heart, this disposition of happy resignation: "O Lord God, in the simplicity of my heart I have joyfully offered all these things . . . keep this will. Alleluia!" The Alleluia is added here today, exceptionally, as a mark of our extreme joy.

At the *Consecration* the gate of heaven is opened, and the Savior re-enters this House of God. And at the *Communion* today's Gospel becomes full reality. As once with the sinful but repentant publican, He presides at a happy banquet. Our joy at the dedication of our church is now complete, for we ourselves have now become a House of God. And Jesus lays on us the duty of ever preserving in holiness the temple of our heart, as also the temple of our church. "My house shall be called the house of prayer!" And He gives the promise: "Everyone that asks therein receives; he who seeks, finds; and to him who knocks, it shall be opened" (*Communion hymn*).

THE FEAST OF CHRIST THE KING

"I Am a King. My Kingdom Is Not of This World!"

In the troubled times between the two World Wars, Pius XI, in the year 1925, inaugurated a special feast in honor of Christ the King. It was meant to be a warning to all the peoples of the world: Christ is the only Leader to happiness and peace. Had the nations at that time listened to this warning they would have been spared nameless disaster. The destiny of the world depends on its attitude toward Christ the King. The Pope selected for this feast the last Sunday before All Saints' Day because then the ecclesiastical year is virtually at an end. "In this manner the mysteries of the life of Jesus Christ . . . are as it were rounded off and compacted. Before we celebrate the glory of all the saints, the glory of Him who triumphs in all the saints is proclaimed and extolled." The texts of the Mass floodlight from all sides the kingship of Christ and the beauty of His kingdom.

At the *Introit* of the Mass we are witnesses, so to speak, of the triumphant entry into heaven of the transfigured Christ on the day of His Ascension. The angels and saints receive Him with a chorus of jubilation, signifying: truly, Thou art worthy now to be crowned by the Father to be King of heaven and earth. "The lamb that was slain is worthy to receive power and divinity . . . to him be glory and empire for ever and ever. Give to the king, O God, thy justice, and to the king's Son thy judgment!"

After this wonderful vision we beseech the heavenly Father in the *Collect:* Grant that, as in heaven, Thy Son may be acknowledged as King here on earth by all peoples: "Mercifully grant that all the nations of mankind who are torn asunder by the wounds of sin may submit to his most sweet rule." How marvelous it would be to live in an age when the leaders of all the states of the world ruled their peoples in the spirit of Christ!

In the opening words of the *Epistle* we give thanks, with Paul, that we too, by baptism, have become members of the kingdom of Christ. "Giving thanks to God the Father, who hath delivered us from the power of darkness and hath translated us into the kingdom of his Son." In a profound theological exposition the Apostle then presents to our view the various proofs of the kingship of Christ. The manhood of Christ was joined with the divine nature in the one Person of the Son of God. Even as man, He is the Son of God, "the image of the invisible God, the first-born of every creature." Hence all things in heaven and on earth are subject to Him. As the eternal Son of God He is, moreover, the Creator of all things. "All things were created by him and in him." Hence, too, all things are utterly dependent on Him. Finally, He is the Redeemer of all mankind. "He is the head of the body, the Church." Through him all things are reconciled with God, making peace through the blood of his cross." Thus by a threefold title we belong entirely to Christ the King. He is the ruler over all peoples, whose regents must govern in accordance with His commandments. For this He will bring the whole world to account when, at the end of time, He shall appear in kingly power in the clouds of heaven.

Meditating on these profound words of the Apostle we mentally contemplate the universality of the kingship of Christ: "He rules from sea to sea . . . unto the ends of the earth. All things of the earth shall adore him; all nations shall do him service" (*Gradual*). The kingship of Christ is not only universal, but also of eternal duration. "His power is an everlasting power, his kingdom shall not be destroyed. Alleluia!" When, at the end of time, Christ has judged the whole world, He reigns on in heaven for all eternity as King of the angels and saints. At the very moment of His conception in the virgin womb of Mary the angel proclaimed: "Of his Kingdom there shall be no end."

In the *Gospel* Christ Himself speaks of His kingship. Faced with death, and knowing that in a short while He will be scoffed at by the soldiers about His kingship, He declares solemnly before Pilate: "Thou sayest that I am a king." But He adds: "My kingdom is not of this world." Earthly kings are concerned about the welfare of their subjects in this world. The kingdom of Christ looks to the eternal happiness of men. God's kingdom of the Church is a king-dom of a spiritual, supernatural kind. "Entry into this kingdom is effected in baptism through faith and repentance. Its adherents must renounce earthly things, must strive after justice (sanctity), must deny themselves, must carry the cross. Christ founded this kingdom through the shedding of His blood" (Pius XI in the Brief). It is "a kingdom of truth and (divine) life, a kingdom of holiness and grace, a kingdom of justice, of love and of peace" (Preface). Thus the kingdom of Christ is really not of this world. Yet it is in this world. It is a visible kingdom, extending over the whole earth. At its head stands the vicar of Christ, the Pope, in Rome. The separate parts of this kingdom are administered by bishops under the supreme direction of the Pope.

Christ was solemnly proclaimed King of this universal Church by His heavenly Father with the words that we recite in the *Offertory hymn:* "Ask of me — and I will give thee the gentiles for thine inheritance, and the uttermost parts of the earth for thy possession." How could we but be filled with devoted loyalty toward so wonderful, powerful and, at the same time, infinitely gracious a King!

In unimaginable love He comes down at the *Consecration* on to the altar and immolates Himself for us as the eternal kingly High Priest. When, at the Communion, He comes into our breasts, let us proffer our heart to this great and loving King to be the throne of His majesty. O Jesus, be Thou King over all my thoughts, desires and actions. To serve Thee is to rule. "If I knew that there remained in me a single fibre that did not love Thee (O Savior), I yearned to tear it out by force" (Francis de Sales). To Thee do I give myself utterly; dispose of me as Thou wilt. I have no longer any will of my own; do Thou decide all things concerning me and how my life shall run until the last breath that I breathe. If we give ourselves thus to Christ, then one day we shall reign with Christ in heaven for all eternity. Then will be fulfilled the words of the *Communion hymn:* "The Lord shall sit as King for ever; the Lord shall bless his people with peace."

FEAST OF ALL SAINTS

Our Ultimate Goal of Bliss!

IN THE early centuries of Christianity only the martyrs were honored by the Church with feast days of their own. These it was, in those times of great persecutions, that stood out as the heroes of Christendom. Since the fifth century Confessors, Virgins, and holy women also came to be honored as saints. Hence there were soon so many saints that the days of the year no longer sufficed for individual honoring of them. This led of itself to a general Feast of All Saints.

At the end of the ecclesiastical year, in the course of which we have commemorated so many individual saints, we now celebrate "a festival day in honor of all the saints" (Collect). Today is the Harvest Thanksgiving of the Church. It is as if the roof of our church had opened and the saints had floated down into our midst. From the regions of the blessed we hear songs of the homeland, songs of peace and joy. We are in fact joined together in one great community.

Thus we too are filled with holy joy, and, in unison with the angels, we sing: "Let us all rejoice in the Lord, celebrating a festival day in honor of all the saints; at whose solemnity the angels rejoice, and give praise to the Son of God" (*Introit*).

The *Collect* expresses the hope that today not only, as at other times, the special saints of the day, but all the saints in a body, may intercede with God for us poor pilgrims on earth. "By the very force of the numbers of our intercessors, we expect today to receive a superabundance of redemptive grace."

Heart-stirring indeed is the *Lesson* from the Apocalypse. The Apostle John allows us a glimpse into heaven. The curtain is drawn wide and we see "a great multitude, which no man could number, of all nations, and tribes, and peoples, and tongues, standing before the throne [of God] and in the sight of the Lamb [Christ], clothed with white robes and palms in their hands" and singing in union with the angels a hymn of praise to God. They are the descendants of the Jews and of heathendom. For each of the twelve tribes of

178

the Jews a round figure of 12,000 saints ("signed") is mentioned, that is, 144,000 in all. This is meant to convey that the multitude is numberless. How much greater the number of saints from the other peoples! All this makes a number much greater than the Church has canonized or beatified, which comes to barely 2000. Hence we are commemorating today also those whose names are not to be found in the earthly Calendar of Saints but who are, of a certainty, inscribed in the heavenly Book of Life. And among them many also with whom we have ourselves lived. They were flesh of our flesh; they had to face storms and struggles, like ourselves. If these could reach the eternal goal, then why not we? It is not heroic deeds and miracles that make saints, but faithfulness in the small things of life. Today we greet these venerable brothers and sisters in heaven and they greet us in return. "All the saints salute you" (2 Cor. 13:12).

This glimpse into heaven fills us with holy hope: one day I too shall be with them up there. Our thoughts still lingering on what we have beheld, we sing the *Gradual:* Ye saints of heaven, "fear the Lord; for there is no want to them that fear him." This holds good also for us here on earth. Therefore let us confidently "seek the Lord"; then we too "shall not be deprived of any good," and we too shall one day celebrate "All Saints" in heaven. Until that day, however, we shall have much suffering to endure. But the Savior Himself stands at our side, inviting us: "Come to me all you that labor and are heavy laden, and I will refresh you." Filled with confidence we then sing the Alleluia.

Now, in the *Gospel,* the same Savior shows us the way to heaven. It is the way of the Sermon on the Mount. The "Eight Beatitudes" are the golden ladder to heaven with its eight rungs. Frankly, it is a steep and difficult ascent. It means carrying the cross, overcoming self, detaching oneself from the earth and its seductions. Only they who daily mortify their own will shall one day be numbered among the blessed. These are the "poor in spirit," who feel themselves poor and paltry in the sight of God and ascribe all that is good in them to His grace. The "meek," who patiently bear injustice in the spirit of Christ, without giving way to anger. The "mourners," who take no joy in the sinful pleasures of the world but seek their whole comfort only in God. Just as those driven by hunger or thirst crave for food and drink, so these crave for holiness. The "merciful," who see the necessities of their fellow men and, by depriving themselves, come to their aid. The "pure of heart," who carefully avoid not only mortal sins but also deliberate venial sins. The "peacemakers," who, by overcoming their passions, carry peace in their own hearts and bring peace to those around them. The "unjustly persecuted," who for love of Christ even take upon themselves imprisonment and death. To all of these the Savior calls out at the end of the *Gospel:* "Be glad and rejoice, for your reward is very great in heaven."

To the worldly, of course, such a life of sacrifice seems foolish; it makes them sorry for us. But in reality by this seeming death we are traveling the royal way of the cross to Christ in heaven. "The souls of the just [in heaven] are in the hand of God. In the sight of the unwise they seemed to die, but they are in peace. Alleluia" (*Offertory hymn*).

And so today, at the *Consecration,* let us unite ourselves with Christ when He immolates Himself for us. At that solemn moment let us group ourselves around the altar of sacrifice in company with all the saints, adoring, thanking, praising. By His holy Sacrifice and His union with us in *Communion* He gives us the strength faithfully to observe the Eight Beatitudes in our lives. So that even now, in Christian hope, we already feel something of the bliss of heaven, above all at the moment of Communion: "Blessed are the clean of heart . . . the peacemakers . . . they that suffer persecution for justice' sake — theirs [ours] is the kingdom of heaven" (*Communion hymn*).